America's Religions

AMERICA'S RELIGIONS
An Educator's Guide to Beliefs and Practices

Benjamin J. Hubbard
California State University, Fullerton

John T. Hatfield
California State Polytechnic University, Pomona

James A. Santucci
California State University, Fullerton

1997
TEACHER IDEAS PRESS
A Division of
Libraries Unlimited, Inc.
Englewood, Colorado

TEACHER IDEAS PRESS
A Division of
Libraries Unlimited, Inc.
P.O. Box 6633
Englewood, CO 80155-6633
1-800-237-6124
www.lu.com/tip

Production Editor: Kay Mariea
Copy Editor: Jason Cook
Proofreader: Suzanne Hawkins Burke
Indexer: Nancy Fulton
Interior Design and Layout: Pamela J. Getchell

Library of Congress Cataloging-in-Publication Data

Hubbard, Benjamin Jerome.
    America's religions : an educator's guide to beliefs and practices /
Benjamin J. Hubbard, John T. Hatfield, James A. Santucci.
    xxiv, 162 p. 17x25 cm.
    Includes bibliographical references and index.
    ISBN 1-56308-469-4
    1. United States--Religion.   2. Religions--Study and teaching--
United States.   3. Religion in the public schools--United States.
I. Hatfield, John T., 1932-   . II. Santucci, James A. III. Title.
BL2525.H82 1997
200'.973--dc21   97-13949
                                                          CIP

Contents

Foreword

Today's classrooms reflect the increasing diversity in the United States. As we strive to meet our students' academic needs, we have neglected to gain a thorough understanding of students' cultural and religious practices and beliefs. Naturally, the term *religion* sends up red flags when used in association with public education, and rightfully so. The Constitution defines a separation between church and state. We often hear about the ongoing legal battles and controversy involving the church-state issue. Still, we cannot neglect the fact that individual public school sites have student populations that may represent as many as 50 different languages, and this clearly reflects a global population.

Our job as educators is to teach this student population the essential skills needed to become literate readers, literate writers, and independent thinkers. We are responsible for molding our country's next adult generation. Problems arise when our actions as educators unknowingly offend or confuse students by presenting conflicts with their cultural or religious beliefs. When this occurs, we create unnecessary problems within our educational system. Many educators have heard the anecdote about the teacher who called a student to his desk with a hand signal, not realizing that this hand signal was a form of disrespect in the student's culture. I myself have heard this story used many times—as incitement for developing a greater awareness and respect of cultural diversity—yet I believe that few teachers are aware of the specific hand gesture or the culture that it offends.

Recently, I became aware of a situation that occurred in my own school district. A male member of a theater group performing at an elementary school assembly went into the audience and sat next to and placed his arm around a female student. This student had recently arrived from Somalia and was dressed in a full head veil. The actor may have thought that he was doing a good deed by involving this particular student in an auditorium of 400 students. Perhaps he thought that his actions, directed at a student who looked different, would help an "outsider" feel more at ease. However, the actor had not realized that this student's attire was, foremost, an indicator of her cultural and religious differences. This young girl was Muslim, and she became so upset (because a male had placed his arm around her) that her mother had to come and remove her from school for the remainder of the day. I am sure the actor meant no harm by choosing this student, but the fact remains that this incident could have been avoided. The purpose of *America's Religions: An Educator's Guide to Beliefs and Practices* is to help develop "trained eyes" so that such incidents are less likely to occur.

In the classroom, I have heard different groups of people referred to as "inconvenient" while a student from one of these groups was present. These inconveniences usually come in the form of special needs based on someone's religious or cultural background. This book will explain the importance of individual customs and beliefs and give teachers concrete information that will help them with classroom management. Teachers are in a powerful position. Students look to teachers as models. I frequently see young students trying to dress like their teacher or use a phrase that the teacher often uses. If a young student looks to you so reverently that he or she wants to dress and talk like you, it is likely that you could make lasting impressions on the student regarding religious issues. This is why cultural and religious diversity in the classroom must be understood, respected, and handled with great care.

I grew up in a rather unusual situation, and I remember the effects it had on me. I attended a public elementary school in Canada where the class began each day by reciting the Lord's Prayer and reading from the New Testament. The Bible was passed around the classroom daily, so that students could read the day's passage aloud. It did not matter whether or not reading from the Bible was part of your religious background—this was simply something the class did. There were, of course, students that did not believe in what they were being asked to do, and parents who did not believe in what their children were being asked to do. Consequently (though unnecessarily), there was tension in the classroom.

Students should feel that school is a safe environment where powerful learning is to take place. School is a place of education, not indoctrination. By familiarizing ourselves with people's customs, we as educators can fulfill our role while maintaining the proper level of respect for all cultures and religions in the classroom.

Think of this book as a dictionary of religion and culture. Within its pages are clearly stated definitions of the many different cultures, religions, and branches of religions you may be encountering in your classroom. Use this book to familiarize yourself with religious beliefs and practices. This will help you avoid conflict with your students and their families. This book also helps explain the "fine legal line" between *teaching* and *celebrating* religion in the classroom, an issue that is the focus of many court battles.

As a former public school teacher and presently a school administrator, I fully appreciate the time constraints teachers face. Curricula, teachers, students, and administrators change; and somehow through all this change, we must continue to deliver a quality program. You have a new book in front of you, but to devote time to it means taking time from another area. I understand that frustration. What I can tell you is that the information you acquire from this book should help save you time in the future. Your time savings will come in the form of a well-tuned classroom where students are respected and experience a safe learning environment. This in turn can keep teachers from entering into unprofessional and embarrassing situations that often lead to time-consuming conferences with parents and administrators.

Finally, as an added benefit, I offer to you the following service: If you encounter a question about the religious practices of students that is not covered in this book, you may send your question to the Production Editor (Kay Mariea) at Teacher Ideas Press or to Dr. Hubbard at the address below. You will receive a response to your question, and it may be used in a future edition of this book.

Dr. Benjamin Hubbard
Department of Religious Studies
California State University
Fullerton, CA 72634-9480
(714) 773-3452
E-mail: bhubbard@fullerton.edu

David A. Hubbard, M.P.A., M.S.
School Administrator, Highland Elementary School
Riverside, California

Preface

Should religion be discussed in public schools? It could well be argued that the United States is the most multicultural and multi-religious society that has ever existed. From around the world, people have been coming here in ever increasing variety, bringing with them religious traditions both familiar and exotic. This mix of religions, bringing with it the inevitable tensions that arise when people with different beliefs live together, as well as fertile opportunities that may ensue when people learn to reach out across their differences, makes modern America an exciting and dramatic stage on which to encounter religion.

At the same time, this proliferation of religions has brought about considerable confusion. In response, some people have turned to the secular world and dismissed religion as hopelessly outdated. Others have sought to simplify their confusion by adhering to one religion and shutting out the rest. Still others have tried to find common threads that would tie together the diversity into one synthetic religion. Amidst this sometimes bewildering variety of opinion, the public schools have been caught in a dilemma. On the one hand, teachers want students to learn about the many cultures that constitute the United States; but on the other hand, teachers feel constrained by legislation and court rulings that seem to prohibit teaching religion. Publishers of school textbooks typically avoid altogether the subject of religion. What are teachers to do?

Although it might be tempting simply to avoid teaching about religion, many teachers have said that if only they had resources to help them develop lessons, they would be more comfortable with religion. Also, if only they had a readily available guide to the practices and beliefs of the students in their classrooms, if only they knew just a bit more about how to handle expressions of religion in public schools, they would be willing to take the challenge.

This book provides just such a resource. However, this book is not just for teachers, though they are the primary audience. News reporters, for example, know that they cannot represent the news fully without including the religious dimension. The reading public can hardly be expected to understand current world events without some knowledge of religious traditions. People who work in international business and overseas relief organizations, government, tourism, scientific and educational fields, and international exchange programs, as well as social workers, therapists, health care professionals, and attorneys, all encounter unfamiliar religious beliefs and practices regularly. These people and others may find in this book useful information to help them understand the religious backgrounds of people they encounter in their everyday work.

Religions Discussed

Including each and every religion one might encounter in the United States would make this book too large and unwieldy. We have used three criteria in deciding what traditions to include. First, the religion must be a living tradition flourishing in the United States. Second, it must command nationwide attention or be of national interest. Third, it must be among those religions encountered in the public school system.

Discussion Format

Each chapter is subdivided as follows: Origins, Beliefs, Sacred Books/Scriptures, Practices, Main Subgroups, Common Misunderstandings and Stereotypes, Classroom Concerns, Population Data, Notes, and Further Reading. Thus, the reader will be able to find information quickly and compare facts about different religions (e.g., population data on Muslims and Buddhists). The sections on origins and beliefs are as brief as possible, while those on common misunderstandings and stereotypes and classroom concerns have been given special attention.

Authors' Point of View

We have written this book from the point of view of sympathetic observers who are trying to understand religious traditions from the inside. However odd, strange, or different a religion may appear to those who are outsiders, it is not our role to judge whether it is true or false. Rather, we have tried to let each religion tell its own story.

For us, this is an ongoing effort to provide the most accurate and up-to-date information possible about the world's religions, as they are found in the United States. Inevitably, we may distort or misrepresent. No offense is intended, and we are open to suggestions for improvement. Please send your comments to us through Dr. Hubbard (see address in "Foreword") or the publisher.

At the end of each chapter, the initials of the contributor are provided: JH (John Hatfield), BH (Benjamin Hubbard), JS (James Santucci).

Dating System

Instead of B.C. (Before Christ) and A.D. (*Anno Domini*, Latin for "In the year of the Lord"), we have adopted the more neutral and inclusive B.C.E. (Before the Common Era; i.e., before the era *common* to Jewish and Christian peoples); and C.E. (Common Era). The dates remain the same, only the designations (B.C. = B.C.E.; A.D. = C.E.) are different. Of course, we could have chosen the Muslim or some other dating system, but B.C.E./C.E. is widely used by most religion scholars.

Pronunciation of Foreign Words

We have developed a common-sense pronunciation system whereby unfamiliar terms are phonetically spelled in brackets following the word, with capital letters designating stress. For example, the word *Christmas* would be followed by this pronunciation: [KRISS-muss]. We hope this will help the reader to feel more at ease when trying to pronounce unfamiliar words, and we are certain that students, particularly those from minority religious backgrounds, will appreciate your effort.

Acknowledgments

We must first acknowledge teacher David Hubbard (the son of Benjamin Hubbard), who suggested to his father that a book of this nature would greatly benefit public school teachers. Each year, David's classes—and those of thousands of teachers across the nation—were becoming more multicultural and, consequently, more multi-religious. Yet, there was no resource available to guide teachers through the customs and practices associated with particular religious backgrounds and to help them avoid offending their students, albeit unwittingly. Thus was born the idea of writing a book to fill this need. Not only did David Hubbard come up with the idea for this book, he read the entire manuscript from the perspective of a public school teacher, removing jargon that only a religion scholar would understand and editing the manuscript for greater clarity. We are very much in his debt.

Benjamin Hubbard wishes to express his thanks to his two collaborators, John Hatfield and James Santucci, who took his dream to heart and produced chapters full of accurate information and keen insight.

We would like to thank the following experts for their help in reading and suggesting improvements to various chapters in the book: Susan Garber (Introduction), Dr. Jessie Owen Smith (African American Christianity), Dr. Fazlollah Berdjis (The Baha'i Faith), Dr. Ananda Guruge (Buddhism), Mary Roddie and Robert Gilbert (Christian Science), Pandit Dr. Justin O'Brien (Hinduism), Imam Dr. Muzammil Siddiqi and Susan Douglas (Islam), Rev. Bruce Montgomery (Jehovah's Witnesses), Rabbi Allen Krause (Judaism), Dr. Ronald Peterson (Mormonism), Dr. Charles Frazee (Orthodox Christianity), Dr. Richard Johnson (Protestant Christianity), Dr. Daniel Brown (Roman Catholic Christianity), Dr. Gerald Larue (Secular Humanism), Dr. Dalton Baldwin (Seventh-day Adventists) and Dr. James Nelson (Unitarian Universalism).

We express our gratitude to Dr. Joseph Annicharico, Assistant Superintendent of the Ramona (California) Unified School District, for allowing us to reproduce in Appendix A the policy statement "Recognition of Religious Beliefs and Customs."

We also want to thank Ms. Jo Ann Robinson and Ms. Giulii Kraemer of the Department of Religious Studies at California State University, Fullerton, for clerical support. Benjamin Hubbbard would like to thank Judy Hubbard for moral support and frequent reminders to complete the book before the turn of the century.

Introduction

Presented here is an overview of the key issues a classroom teacher is liable to encounter when teaching about religion or when dealing with questions or situations related to religion, and specific suggestions for dealing with them. The issues are arranged according to the eight topics discussed for each religion.

Origins

The United States always has been a religiously plural nation. In the twentieth century, the number of religions practiced in the United States has increased more than ever before. There are several reasons for this proliferation in the United States: (1) Generally, Americans regard religion as a matter of personal conscience and choice and believe that people should be free to choose which religion to practice or to choose not to practice religion. (2) Because the First Amendment—ratified in 1791—separated church from state, there is no central religious authority for the country. (3) Immigrants have brought their religions from all parts of the world. (4) No one church or religion is dominant over another.

The establishment and implementation of the principles of the First Amendment have involved controversy and struggle, which continue today. This momentous effort is part of the history of the United States, a unique experiment in freedom. If we overlook the connection between this country's history and its religious traditions, we cannot possibly understand what it means to be American.

Beliefs

The First Amendment to the Constitution begins: "Congress shall make no law respecting an establishment of religion, or prohibiting the free exercise thereof." Charles Haynes, of The Freedom Forum First Amendment Center at Vanderbilt University, has led the way in understanding how to use the first principles articulated in the Constitution to guide educational policies and practices about religion. In *Finding Common Ground*, he writes that the fundamental question in the modern United States is: "How to live with our deepest differences?"[1] The First Amendment's religion section has two clauses that protect the exercise of freedom of conscience for people of all faiths or none. The Establishment Clause protects citizens from religious persecution because no one religion is sponsored ("established") by the government, and the Free Exercise clause guarantees the right of citizens to "reach, hold, exercise or change beliefs freely."[2]

In the United States, then, you can practice or not practice whatever religion you choose. The two clauses together provide the principles by which we can learn to live with our deepest differences and celebrate our religious diversity. Our common ground is a shared understanding of the "place of religion in public life and of the guiding principles by which people with deep religious differences can contend robustly but civilly with each other."[3] Because our religious liberty is a right extended to everyone, we need to be particularly vigilant in protecting that right for others so that we may enjoy it ourselves.

Sacred Books/Scriptures

Many religious traditions are based on written records—books, scrolls, tapestries, tablets, clay vessels, and the like. Given the prominence of written records in most of the religions discussed in this book, we decided to make this one of the elements in our summaries of the various religions. It is important to understand, however, that traditions without scriptures (e.g., Native American) are also worthy of study.

Practices

> "It might well be said that one's education is not complete without a study of comparative religion or the history of religion and its relationship to the advancement of civilization. It certainly may be said that the Bible is worthy of study for its literary and historic qualities. Nothing we have said here indicates that such a study of the Bible or of religion, when presented objectively as part of a secular program of education, may not be effected consistently with the First Amendment."[4]

While the First Amendment provides the guiding principles for religion in public schools, the Supreme Court, in two significant decisions, has interpreted how these principles may be applied. With regard to the Establishment Clause, the Lemon Test (*Lemon v. Kurtzman*, 1971) stipulates that a negative answer to any of the following three questions makes a law relating to religion unconstitutional: "(1) Does the law, or other government action, have a bona fide secular or civic purpose? (2) Does the primary effect neither advance nor inhibit religion? In other words, is it neutral? (3) Does the law avoid excessive governmental entanglement with religion?"[5] If all three questions can be answered in the affirmative, the law is legal. Because public schools represent the government, their policies and legal positions must pass the Lemon Test.

With regard to the Free Exercise clause, the Sherbert Test (*Sherbert v. Verner*, 1963) stipulates that citizens—in attempting to practice their religion—can claim protection if their actions "(1) are motivated by a sincere religious belief, and (2) have been substantially burdened by the government."[6] It also says that government can prevail, nevertheless, if it can show that "(1) it is acting in furtherance of a 'compelling state interest,' and (2) it has pursued that interest in the manner least restrictive, or least burdensome, to religion."[7] Under this test, sincerely religious students may pray silently in class without fear of being "burdened," or restricted, by the government (school), but they cannot pray in a way that will interfere with the government's "interest" of conducting an orderly class or in ways that would coerce or harass others. These guidelines will also help teachers decide how to treat religious holidays in the classroom; where and how to teach creationism;[8] how to deal with challenges brought by parents; and how to treat particular religious practices, such as not saluting the flag.

The First Amendment provides that religions shall be neither advocated nor opposed, that fairness and neutrality should prevail. Fairness means that religions should be taught without injecting personal beliefs. This can be done by attribution ("most Hindus believe . . ."). Fairness involves a critical and careful approach that includes the positive and negative aspects of a religion. A stance of fairness will acknowledge the adverse effects religions have had on history as well as their uplifting and beneficial contributions. Fairness says that we should teach not only about religion, but also about the absence of religion (often called Humanism, which is included in this book). Fairness means not making judgments about the comparative worth of religions. Each religion should be respected in its own right.

Fairness dictates that we avoid "explaining away" religion. For example, we should not teach the view that all religions are the same; or that they are merely outmoded ways of thinking; or that they are all relative to one another; or that one is better than another. These views make assumptions about religion that are not factually demonstrable. Neither is it enough simply to tolerate other religions, because toleration too often is a patronizing stance in which those in power "put up with" others. Fairness means, rather, a positive respect for religious difference, as well as a desire to understand the way each religion understands truth, goodness, justice, and so forth. It means an appreciation of how religions affect the lives of their followers. The goal should always be to understand how the religion understands itself.

Main Subgroups

The variety of religions in the United States is greater than at any time or place in history. This, together with the unique experiment of making religion a constitutionally guaranteed choice, has given religion in the United States a very special flavor. We have supplied chapters on religions that are widely practiced in the United States. You are liable to encounter many of these religions in your classroom:

The Baha'i Faith

Buddhism

Chinese Religions (Confucianism and Taoism)

Christianity (Orthodox, Roman Catholicism, Protestantism; and African American Christianity; Christian Science; Mormonism/Church of Jesus Christ of Latter-day Saints; Jehovah's Witnesses; Seventh-day Adventists)

Hinduism

Islam

Jainism

Judaism

Native American Religions

Sikhism

Unitarian Universalism

We have also provided chapters on the following:

Fundamentalism

Secular Humanism/Atheism

New Age Religion

We have not included Shinto (the nature-oriented religion of Japan) or Zoroastrianism/ Parsees (an originally Persian religion—most of whose followers now live in India— with a monotheistic God, Ahura Mazda, who will eventually defeat the evil force, Ahriman) because of the small number of adherents in the United States.

Common Misunderstandings and Stereotypes

Some teachers may be reluctant to teach about religions for fear of making mistakes or offending someone. However, when teachers are making an honest and sympathetic effort to portray a religion, students and their parents seldom take offense and often will provide clarification.

Occasionally, teachers are challenged by parents who either believe religion should not be taught at all or want their faith taught rather than the religion currently being presented in class. When teachers take time to explain exactly what they are doing—teaching *about* religion as it occurs in the curriculum or in the calendar (e.g., at Christmas, the Buddha's birthday, etc.), without advocating any one religious point of view, and being neutral and fair toward all religions—parents usually are willing to forgo their disagreements in favor of education.

Some teachers may feel that their own religious convictions prevent them from teaching about other religions. They need to understand their responsibilities as public servants subject to the provisions of the Constitution. Personal convictions, whether for or against religion, should not be allowed to dominate. Nevertheless, this does not mean teachers cannot reveal their convictions to the class. What this does mean is that teachers should state their convictions only as *personal* beliefs, making it clear that the task of the teacher is to present fairly the various religions of the world. One important caution: Because students in the elementary grades are very impressionable, there is a danger—they may assume that your beliefs should be true for them as well.

Classroom Concerns

Most teachers agree that students learn more when they are actively involved. Because there is a fine line between explaining a particular symbol or ritual and actually using it religiously, greater care than usual should be taken when dealing with religious activities. The secular and historical nature of the study should be carefully established so that students of any faith (or none) will not be put in a position of betraying their own faith. In establishing the factual and historical setting, students may read and study sacred literature as dramatic events, such as the Exodus of the Jews from Egypt. Then, dramatic presentations can represent the religious life of people, rather than imitate religious ritual. An appropriate time for such activities is in connection with the calendar of religious holidays that many school districts establish for study. Of course, students should understand that they may be excused from such activity if it compromises their own beliefs or values.

We suggest that teachers avoid asking students about their personal religious beliefs. However, on their own initiative, students may make reports, write papers, create artwork, and do homework about their faith. When relevant, they may express their religious beliefs in the course of classroom discussions. It is also permissible to invite knowledgeable adults to discuss religious topics in class, so long as they do it in a non-coercive, non-proselytizing manner. The teacher may make a general invitation to the class, asking for names of adults, including parents and community members, who might be available to speak about their religions. Suggested guidelines for topics include the following questions: Is it permitted by the Constitution? Is it educationally sound and culturally sensitive? Is it appropriate to the class level? Does it recognize that there is more than one view on any issue? Does it avoid generalizing and making "universal" (stereotypical) statements?

Art and music are effective sources of instruction in religious traditions. Artifacts and symbols may be displayed and used in instruction, with the understanding that they are not being used in a religious manner. Music may be studied to learn about religious attitudes and feelings. Architecture, painting, calligraphy, sculpture, and ceramics are vivid media for teaching about religions. In addition, students may draw, paint, sculpt, compose, or construct artifacts, music, and symbols as a way of learning about religions. As with plays, students should understand that they may be excused from these activities if their beliefs or values will be compromised. Finally, food associated with religious holidays (e.g., potato pancakes, or *latkes*, in connection with the Jewish festival of Hanukkah) might be brought to school, or even cooked at school if facilities are available.

Fundamentalists, whether Christian, Muslim, or Hindu, should not be portrayed as fanatics or "Bible thumpers." Stereotypes abound on both sides, with liberals being portrayed as relativists or "do-gooders." We need to understand all points of view, without expecting that anyone must change. Deeply held religious convictions give meaning and purpose to people's lives. For this reason, people often have a desire to tell others what they have experienced. In this regard, it is possible that a well-meaning student or parent from one of these traditions may try to proselytize in class or invite religious spokespersons to do so. It would then be necessary to mention discreetly that the First Amendment prohibits such activity.

Different religions often have different moral views, especially on issues of sex, abortion, drugs, warfare, and the environment. The First Amendment protects the right of all Americans to express their views. Within reason, this is true in the classroom as well. Sometimes, when students have had instruction at home or at their places of worship, they may become disinterested in the classroom lesson or raise questions about it. Usually, it is enough to mention that there are different ways of thinking about questions of morality, and we need to look at all sides. A variety of views should be encouraged as a way of learning how people with deeply held, but different, religious and moral convictions can live together.

To achieve the best situation for teaching about religion, all those who have an interest, positive or negative, should be included—parents, teachers, administrators, and especially school board members. When all points of view are heard, and when clear and positive policies are established, there will be fewer conflicts, and conflicts that do arise will be treated in a civil manner. In Appendix A, we have provided a model policy on religion in the public school: "Ramona [California] Unified School District Policy Instruction: Recognition of Religious Beliefs and Customs."

Religious expression in school is not prohibited under present law, although it may be controlled as a matter of fairness. Students may pray, read sacred scriptures, discuss and write about religious topics, meet in groups for religious activities, wear religious garments, distribute religious literature, be released for off-campus religious activities during the school day, and be excused from lessons and activities that are contrary to the teachings of their religion. The only restrictions are: (1) these activities cannot interfere with the normal processes of instruction, and (2) they cannot be conducted in a way that would coerce or harass others. What is prohibited by law is state sponsorship or initiation of religious (or anti-religious) activities. For example, the school cannot sponsor or initiate celebrations of religious holidays, although teachers may teach about them, and the school can celebrate the more secular aspects of religious holidays. These secular aspects might include the dreidel game associated with Hanukkah, the Christmas tree, Easter eggs, Tibetan mandalas, Indian (South Asian) dances, the Japanese zodiacal sign, money exchanges in connection with Chinese New Year, roasting corn in Native American style, Hatha yoga (breathing and posture techniques), etc. Perhaps the most difficult challenge for the typical teacher is how to recognize Christmas and Easter in a manner that is informative yet not a veiled worship service.

Population Data

In 1990–91, Kosmin and Lachman[9] conducted a survey of 113,000 randomly selected adults from across the nation, the largest survey of its type this century. They found that 86.2 percent of this country's adult population was Christian, 8.2 percent had no religion, 3.3 percent belonged to other faiths, and 2.3 percent refused to answer. Some scholars have raised questions about the accuracy of the survey results as they apply to the non-Christian religions. For example, Kosmin and Lachman report that there are 527,000 adult Muslims in the United States. Even if we double this number to account for Muslim children, the number of Muslims would be far less than the total reported by Muslim researchers. Some of these scholars have theorized that Muslims contacted in the survey either listed themselves as Christians or refused to answer because of their minority status and the strong anti-Muslim sentiments in this country. By contrast, the total number of Jewish adults (3,137,000) corresponds closely with the results of a 1990 survey sponsored by the Council of Jewish Federations, which listed the total Jewish population (adults and children) at 5.5 million. A scientific study of the nation's Muslim population—and of other minority religions—is needed to clarify the discrepancy.

—J.H. and B.H.

Notes

1. Charles Haynes, ed., *Finding Common Ground: A First Amendment Guide to Religion and Public Education* (Nashville, TN: The Freedom Forum First Amendment Center at Vanderbilt University, 1994), sec. 1.2.

2. Ibid., sec. 2.3.

3. Ibid.

4. Supreme Court Associate Justice Tom Clark, *Abington v. Schempp*, 1963.

5. Haynes, *Finding Common Ground*, sec. 4.5.

6. Ibid.

7. Ibid., 4.6.

8. Creationism, or creation science, attempts to establish scientifically that the world was created out of nothing in six days, about 10,000 years ago. See the chapter "Fundamentalism."

9. Barry A. Kosmin and Seymour P. Lachman, *One Nation Under God: Religion in Contemporary American Society* (New York: Harmony Books, 1993), 1–17.

Further Reading

Haynes, Charles, ed. *Finding Common Ground: A First Amendment Guide to Religion and Public Education*. Nashville, TN: The Freedom Forum First Amendment Center at Vanderbilt University, 1994.

Haynes, Charles. *Religion in American History: What to Teach and How*. Alexandria, VA: Association for Supervision and Curriculum Development, 1990.

Nord, Warren. *Religion and American Education: Rethinking a National Dilemma*. Chapel Hill, NC: University of North Carolina Press, 1995.

The nine-pointed star of the Baha'i Faith represents the numerical value of the Arabic word baha'i, meaning "Glory of God." In Arabic, as in Hebrew, every letter of the alphabet is assigned a numeric value (e.g., a = 1, b = 2, etc.).

The Baha'i Faith

Origins

The Baha'i [ba-HAI] Faith officially began in 1863 in Baghdad, Iraq, under Mirza Husayn Ali Nuri, known as Baha'u'llah [bah-HA-u-lah] (Persian for "splendor of God"), who claimed to be the "manifestation of God," another revealer of divine truth following in the tradition of Moses, Jesus, and Muhammad. He had been part of a movement within Shi'i Islam, Babism, begun by the Bab (Arabic for "gateway"), Mirza (Siyyid) Ali Muhammad, who claimed to be the twelfth imam (in Shi'i Islam, imams are spiritual successors of Muhammad who interpret religious truth for their age). He had disappeared centuries earlier and was to return as the Mahdi [MEH-dee], a messianic figure who would purify Islam. The Bab was executed in 1850, but not before proclaiming that another would follow him and be the prophet of a new, universal religion. Two years later, while imprisoned in the so-called Black Pit of Tehran, Baha'u'llah received his call to be God's prophet for the modern age.

After a period during which descendants of Baha'u'llah succeeded him in leading the movement, the Council of the Hands of the Cause took over leadership from 1957 to 1962 and was succeeded by the current International or Universal House of Justice. The Council is elected every five years and is headquartered in Haifa, Israel.

1

Beliefs

The Baha'i Faith is monotheistic in the tradition of Judaism, Christianity, and Islam. The Baha'is hold that all religions are true because they come from the same divine source. It thus promotes mutual respect and reconciliation between the world's religions, and world peace. Baha'u'llah is the most recent messenger from God. There is, consequently, a strong missionary tradition among Baha'is inspired by the work of the Baha'u'llah's son, Abbas Effendi, who made missionary journeys to Egypt, Europe, and North America.

The Baha'is believe in continuous divine revelation, so that each age requires a new message. In fact, revelation will never be complete because divine truth is limitless. Even the Baha'i Faith itself will eventually be superseded—though not for a thousand years.

The Baha'is hold that science and religion must cooperate because their claims balance each other. Any religion that states something contrary to science is distorting the truth, according to the religion.

The Baha'i Faith stresses equality between men and women. Abdu'l-Baha (surname of Abbas Effendi) wrote in 1912

> When perfect equality shall be established between men and women, peace may be realized for the simple reason that womankind in general will never favor warfare. Women will not be willing to allow those whom they have so tenderly cared for to go to the battlefield. When they shall have a vote, they will oppose any cause of warfare.[1]

Sacred Books/Scriptures

From 1852 to 1877, Baha'u'llah was either imprisoned or living in exile. During this time he began writing the Baha'i scripture, the Kitab-al-aqdas (Arabic for "The Most Holy Book"), which he completed in 1884. He also wrote 100 volumes that explain the faith's teachings.

Practices

Although the Baha'i Faith has no public or private rites or sacraments, it requires its followers to pray daily, to fast (much as Muslims do during Ramadan; see the chapter "Islam") during one of the 19 months in the Baha'i calendar, and to abstain from alcoholic beverages. There are no clergy to conduct worship services, which are usually held in a member's home and include prayer and readings from the Kitab-al-aqdas and other scriptures. In place of local houses of worship, Baha'i followers have erected on five continents magnificent places of worship open to people of all faiths. The North American center is in Wilmette, Illinois, the Asian in Haifa, Israel.

The Baha'is observe several holidays, including:

Naw Ruz. The Baha'i and Iranian new year, celebrated March 21.

Ridvan. A celebration of the religion's founding, when Baha'u'llah revealed himself to his followers. Work is suspended on the first, ninth, and twelfth days of the celebration, April 21–May 2.

Martyrdom of the Bab. A commemoration of the day Baha'u'llah's forerunner was put to death by a firing squad, celebrated July 9.

Birth of the Bab. October 20.

Birth of Baha'u'llah. November 12.

Main Subgroups

It does not appear that there are any significant divisions within the Baha'i Faith.

Common Misunderstandings and Stereotypes

"Baha'i is a type of Islam."
Although the Baha'i Faith developed out of the Shi'i branch of Islam (compare Christianity's evolution from Judaism), it is an independent religion.

Classroom Concerns

The Baha'i Faith is generally not well known in the United States. However, Baha'i children should be accorded respect and recognition (including the mention of the holidays noted in "Practices" above) in light of the noble principles—such as tolerance, peacemaking, and women's rights—that the religion promotes. The Baha'is have been severely persecuted in Iran since the Shah's overthrow in 1978 and the establishment of an Islamic theocracy.

Population Data

There are about 5 million Baha'i followers in the world, including 110,000 in the United States.

—B.H.

Notes

1. Quoted in William A. Young, *The World's Religions: Worldviews and Contemporary Issues* (Englewood Cliffs, NJ: Prentice Hall, 1995), 393.

Further Reading

Esslemont, J. E. *Baha'u'llah and the New Era*. Wilmette, IL: Baha'i Publishing Trust, 1970.

The symbol of Buddhism is the wheel of dharma (Truth, or the teaching or doctrine encompassing Truth), first introduced after the Buddha's Awakening in the First Sermon, entitled "The Turning of the Wheel of Dharma."

Buddhism

Origins

Buddhism arises out of the experience and teaching of an historical figure who lived 2,500 years ago. His family name was Gautama, but a number of titles and epithets describing his spiritual nature and accomplishments were claimed either by Gautama or by his followers: the Buddha (The Awakened One), Siddhârtha [sid-HAHR-tah] (He Who Has Achieved His Goal), Tathâgata (Thus Come, or Thus Gone), and Shâkyamuni (The Sage of the Shâkyas). Most scholars place his birth at about 563 B.C.E. and death at about 483 B.C.E., but there is some consensus among today's scholars that he may have lived between 480 and 400 B.C.E. Born to a king or chieftain of the Shâkya tribe near what is today the Indian-Nepali border, Gautama, when he was still a young man of 29, renounced his birthright, wife, and infant son and chose to become a wandering ascetic (one who practices self-denial) in search of the ultimate Truth about existence and an escape from suffering. He sought the answer for six years before experiencing, at age 35, ultimate freedom from suffering.

Following this "awakening," or *Nirvâna* [near-VAH-nah], the Buddha chose to lead the life of a teacher "for the profit, benefit, and happiness of gods and men."[1] After serving as a teacher for 45 years, he died, or as Buddhists would describe it, achieved the ultimate or final awakening,

4

Parinirvâna—emancipation. To many Buddhists, the Buddha is considered to be an historical figure who accomplished the extraordinary feat of discovering and realizing the highest Truth and sharing this insight with those who sought his counsel. His most important function, therefore, was that of a teacher. This is the view of the Theravâda [terra-VA-dah] school (see "Main Subgroups" below). There has always been a tendency, however, to elevate the Buddha to superhuman status. This tendency was resisted in the Theravâda tradition but accepted in the later, more liberal, Mahâyâna [ma-HAH-YAH-nah] tradition (see "Main Subgroups" below).

Beliefs

The teachings of the Buddha center around insight into the nature of suffering and how to end it. The earliest texts containing these teachings were written three centuries after he died. There is, nonetheless, a fair amount of certainty that the teachings of the Four Noble Truths and Noble Eightfold Path were, in some form or another, original teachings of the Buddha.

The Four Noble Truths state that (1) all of humanity is in a state of suffering or disharmony, expressed specifically as physical, mental, and existential (i.e., birth, aging, and death) suffering; (2) this situation has its origin in a thirst, or excessive and uncontrollable desire, for sensual experience and pleasure, continued existence, and even non-existence or annihilation; (3) this suffering can be stopped by following a path or method designed to achieve this result; and (4) the method the Buddha urged his disciples to follow to achieve the end of suffering, or *Nirvâna*, is the Noble Eightfold Path.

The eight steps of the Noble Eightfold Path are subdivided into three areas of cultivation: of insight, or wisdom; of morality; and of the mind through meditation. Thus the first two steps—*right views* and *right intention*—reflect the cultivation of wisdom; the next three—*right speech*, *right action*, and *right career*—reflect the cultivation of morality; and the last three—*right effort*, *right mindfulness*, and *right concentration*—reflect the cultivation of mind. Employing a medical model, the Buddha is viewed as a doctor who diagnoses the problem that afflicts all humanity and sets forth a cure.

Although the Buddha incorporated the doctrines of *karma*, rebirth, and the existence of various divine and demonic beings from Brahmanism, the dominant or mainstream religion of northern India, he rejected other elements of this religion. The Buddha rejected the most important religious activity of the time, ritual action, specifically those rituals described in the Vedas, the sacred text of Hinduism/Brahmanism. In addition to the Vedic ritual practices, the so-called low arts—such as astrology and palmistry—were also rejected. The basis of society itself was challenged. During the time of the Buddha, four classes were recognized: the brahmins, who regarded themselves as the most prestigious and important class because of their knowledge of the rituals, which in turn controlled the cosmos; administrators and warriors; the farmer/commercial class; and the serfs, or peasants, who served the other classes. This system, based on birth, was unacceptable to the Buddha, who argued that merit, not birth, defined a person's worth.

What was truly revolutionary, however, was the Buddha's rejection of these bedrocks of Hindu philosophy: (1) the Self as the permanent, unchanging life force that was the font of ultimate knowledge for the individual; and (2) the Brahman (Godhead) as the permanent, unchanging, transcendent, unknowable Supreme Force, which both lay beyond the cosmos and was the source of the cosmos. If one rejects these notions, nothing can be permanent and eternal: soul, self, God(s), heaven, hell, or anything within the cosmos.

It is this acceptance of the impermanence of everything, not only of those objects that exist outside of us but also of those elements that comprise the individual, that defines the purpose of Buddhist teaching: to overcome the tenacious grasping after material and mental realm that we mistake as the source of the permanent and unchanging. This impermanence of everything is the source of an unbalanced and unstable existence and experience that constantly impels us to desire things that we do not possess or, once a thing is in our possession, constantly to fear losing it. Indeed, nothing can be possessed because there is no thing that exists unto itself, for there is no substance or essence, no permanent model or ideal that underlies the material and mental realms. The natural consequence to the teachings of impermanence and no-self is that there is no personhood, only a bundle of physical and mental phenomena.

The tenets of Buddhism include: (1) We exist in a condition of dysfunctionality, constantly grasping after whatever we think will make us permanently happy, not mindful that there is nothing that can give us perfect and constant contentment simply because there is nothing that is permanent in this world. (2) The Noble Eightfold Path represents a regimen that avoids an addiction to self-torment—standard practice among the ascetics (practitioners of extreme penitence) of the Buddha's time—as much as it avoids the opposite extreme, an addiction to sensual pleasures. (3) Meditation is the primary practice that overcomes the ills of human condition. It consists of calming the mind (compare to the practice of yoga in Hinduism) and practicing "insight" meditation, in which the mind actively observes all bodily and mental processes. Out of such practices, insight-knowledge, that is, knowledge of the nature of things as they truly are, is gradually developed until there is an ultimate breakthrough: *Nirvâna*, the transcendence of greed, hatred, and delusion.

The importance of pursuing such demanding and time-consuming practices helps to explain why early Buddhism and the Buddhism of South and Southeast Asia, Theravâda Buddhism, is presented more as a monastic religion rather than as a religion of the masses. As a result, the Sangha [SUNG-gha]—the monastic community of monks and, previously, nuns—is given more importance than the ordinary lay community in achieving the goal set forth by the Buddha.

Sacred Books/Scriptures

The sacred compositions of Buddhism are vast in number and composed in many languages. The oldest collection surviving to this day is the Pâli canon (Pâli is a literary language spoken at the time of the Buddha), originating in what was to become the Theravâda tradition. The earliest compositions in the canon were based on the words of the Buddha, though they were not necessarily his exact words. These compositions were called *sûtras* (discourses or scriptures), usually of the Buddha but also of some of his disciples. A later section was added to the canon that presented an analysis of the teachings in the earlier compositions. Around the first century B.C.E., the canon was committed to writing in the island nation of Sri Lanka.

The Pâli canon is divided into *pitakas* (baskets): the Vinaya Pitaka contains the rules for the monks and nuns of the monastic community; the Sutta Pitaka gives the teaching of the Buddha; and the Abhidhamma Pitaka discusses, through various analytical methods, the teaching (*dhamma*, Sanskrit *dharma*) on the factors of experience (*dhammas*).

Authoritative and influential texts also originated within the Mahâyâna and Vajrayâna [vuhj-ruh-YAH-nah] (see "Main Subgroups" below) Buddhist traditions. Many of the texts were known as *sûtras*, like the Pâli texts mentioned above, because they were considered the Buddha's own words. In the Mahâyâna tradition, *sûtras* made their appearance as early as the first century B.C.E., and they continued to be written until the eighth century C.E. Most prominent are the Wisdom Sûtras, of which there are longer and shorter versions (including the Diamond and Heart Sûtras), the Lotus Sûtra, and the Pure Land Sûtras, to name just a few. Vajrayâna, or the "Apocalyptic Vehicle," originated with the introduction of new texts known as *tantras* (systems), esoteric (hidden and mysterious) ritual texts dating from the sixth century C.E. onward.

Practices

Buddhism began as a practice designed to overcome any opinion or emotional state that bound one to this world of suffering. Meditation (see "Beliefs" above), in which the mind is in a calm, observant state, is the principal practice of the majority of Buddhists.

Not every Buddhist school practices meditation, however. There is a devotional side to Buddhism: the Pure Land School, for example, emphasizes the recitation of a formula (*nien-fo* [Chinese] or *Nembutsu* [Japanese]): "*na-mo-a-mi-t'o-fo*" [Homage of Amida Buddha]) that will make it possible for one to be reborn in the Western Paradise (a temporary heaven that has no connection to the world of suffering); the Nichiren School emphasizes that its members recite the *daimoku* (sacred phrase) "*Namu myô-hô-ren-ge kyô*" (Homage to the Lotus Sûtra) as encompassing the perfect expression of the Buddhist teaching. For the Vajrayâna, of which Tibetan Buddhism is an example, its monks and nuns practice elaborate rituals with the use of *mantras* (sacred syllables or phrases) and *mudrâs* (hand gestures) to effect a mystical state in the mind. The practices of lay people within the entire Buddhist community mainly involve acts of merit designed to bring about a better existence in a future life, which in turn will eventually lead to final liberation. These acts include offering food and robes to monks, constructing *stupas* or *pagodas* (shrines to the Buddha, sometimes containing his relics), gilding statues of the Buddha with gold leaf, and visiting temples.

Vegetarianism is often associated with Buddhism, but it is not universal. It is a practice of monastics in China but not in Japan.

A Buddhist recitation called "Three Jewels" is common to all Buddhists and is also employed by one who converts to Buddhism: "I take refuge in the Buddha, I take refuge in the Sangha [monastic community], I take refuge in the Dharma [teaching]."

Major Buddhist festivals and holidays include:

Wesak (in the Sri Lankan tradition) or **Visakha Puja** (in the Thai tradition). A celebration of the birth, enlightenment, and *Parinirvâna* of the Buddha. Ceremony is observed on the day of the full moon in May.

Asalha Puja. Commemoration of the Buddha giving his first sermon to his original five disciples. This is held on the full moon day in July.

The Lantern Festival. A festival commemorating the proof that Buddhist sûtras were genuine because they, unlike the scriptures of the Taoists and local deities, did not burn when set afire. The ceremony is observed by Chinese and other Asians on the fifteenth day of the first lunar month. Lamps are lit to symbolize the light of Buddhism.

All Souls' Day. A commemoration of the dead involving the transfer of merit to the ancestors to keep them from becoming malevolent, because souls may become dangerous if not properly treated. Ceremony occurs on the fifteenth day of the seventh lunar month (July or August) and is based on the story of the Arhant (awakened disciple of the Buddha) Maudgalyâyana's search for his mother in hell. Usually, lanterns are placed on small boats and set adrift on a river or other body of water.

New Year's Day. A celebration by Buddhists in the Chinese, Vietnamese, and, in part, Korean communities. According to the Chinese lunar calendar, the celebration takes place around February. Sri Lankans, Thais, Laotians, Burmese, and Cambodians celebrate the new year according to a different calendar, generally on the 13th or 14th of April. This day is considered a good time to perform acts of merit.

Main Subgroups

Preliminary Remarks

Buddhism today is generally identified according to three traditions or *yâna* (vehicles): Theravâda,[2] Mahâyâna, and Vajrayâna. To capture the primary emphasis of each of the three traditions, (1) Theravâda (the Teaching of the Elders) will be referred to as "Individual Vehicle;"[3] (2) Mahâyâna (Great[er] Vehicle) will be called "Universal Vehicle;" and (3) Vajrayâna (Vehicle of the Thunderbolt) will be referred to as "Apocalyptic Vehicle."[4] The term *yâna*, also translated as "career" or "path" (sanskrit, *mârga*), is considered equivalent to Buddhist doctrine. Since the First Sermon of the Buddha was called the "Turning of the Wheel of Dharma," those Buddhists who recognized the Three Vehicles identified them respectively as the First, Second, and Third Turning of the Wheel of Dharma. The First Turning focuses on the Four Noble Truths and Eightfold Noble Path described in the First Sermon of the Buddha; the Second focuses on the Doctrine of Emptiness (the teaching that no thing possesses independence, substantiality, or inherent nature); and the Third focuses on the Buddha-Nature (the teaching that all beings possess the potential of becoming a buddha).

Although Buddhism is identified by non-Buddhists according to vehicle or tradition, few Buddhists except the Theravâdins identify themselves in this manner, for reasons explained below. Rather, it is the lineage or teacher, often called a school or sub-school—a typically South Asian approach that carries over into the Far East and elsewhere—that is the badge of identity. For instance, Mahâyâna Buddhists identify themselves through one of the many schools established in China, Japan, or elsewhere, such as the Pure Land School (stressing the attainment of the Western Paradise through recitation of the name of the Amida Buddha, *"na-mo-a-mi-t'o-fo"*) of the Japanese teacher Honen (1133–1212) or of Shinran (1173–1262); the Ch'an or Zen school (with its emphasis on meditation techniques) of the Japanese teacher Dogen (1200–1253), known as Soto Zen, or the Rinzai Zen school of the Japanese teacher Eisai (1141–1215); or the Nichiren school (inspired by the medieval Buddhist priest Nichiren (1222–1282) who taught that the best practice was the *daimoku "Namu myô-hô-ren-ge kyô."*[5]

Theravâda

Based on the above remarks, Theravâda may be viewed as both a *yâna* (tradition) and a school. As the sole representative of the Individual Vehicle,[6] Theravâda is the predominant form of Buddhism in South Asia (Sri Lanka) and Southeast Asia (Myanmar [Burma], Thailand, Cambodia, and Laos). From a modern-day perspective, it is through the South and Southeast Asian immigrants that Theravâda is represented in the United States and other Western countries. Buddhism began to fragment fairly early in its history. Around 349 B.C.E. the first major schism took place resulting in two divisions: the **Sthavira-vâda** (the Tradition or Doctrine of the Elders) and **Mahâsanghikas** (Those Who Belong to the Great Assembly), with the latter separating from the former, according to the historical accounts. It is generally assumed within Buddhism that the orthodox teaching and monastic discipline developed along Sthavira lines, but even though the Sanskrit compound Sthavira-vâda is equivalent to the Pâli Theravâda, we cannot automatically assume that Theravâda Buddhism today is identical to original Buddhism. We may safely assume, however, that it represents an early strand of Buddhism. Around the time of Ashoka (268–232 B.C.E.), the Theravâda Buddhists identified themselves as **Vibhajyavâdins** (Those Who Distinguish, referring to a method of analysis of distinguishing between those factors of existence or *dharmas* that "exist" and those factors that don't). At least this early, the Theravâdins viewed themselves as a separate school from others that were appearing at this time.

When Ashoka instigated Buddhist missionary activity to foreign lands, it was Theravâda that was established in Sri Lanka with the coming of Ashoka's son, Mahinda, in 243 B.C.E. With the arrival of Theravâda in Sri Lanka, the tradition-school assumes a firm foundation in history, and the Pâli canon was first set down in writing in the first century B.C.E. in an organized fashion.

The practice of Theravâda focuses on the monastic life. The term *sangha* (community) generally refers to the monastic order (*bhikkhu-sangha*). Some monks are "forest-dwelling" monks who live in secluded locales and engage in meditation and ascetic practices (*dhutânga*) such as refusing to eat at the house of a lay person or refusing to dwell in a village or town.[7] They will also preach the Dharma or Buddhist teaching. They follow the traditional rules of the community of monks (*vinaya*) more strictly than the "village monks" who participate in the ceremonial needs of the laity, such as participating in funerals and other ceremonials.

Although a community of nuns (*bhikkhunî-sangha*) existed from the time of the Buddha, it died out in the thirteenth century when Mongols sacked Pagan (Myanmar [Burma]). Recently, communities of nuns taking the first eight precepts (of the traditional 10 of the monks)[8] have been established and are generally independent or attached to monasteries.

Lay persons conduct themselves differently than monastics. For one, it is generally assumed that *Nirvâna* is out of reach for lay persons in this or the next life, so most of their religious activities are designed to gain merit (good karma) to achieve a better, more spiritual present and future life. Nirvâna will be achieved in a more distant lifetime. Acts of merit for the lay community include listening to the Dharma and making donations to the monks and temple. A more intense practice might include taking the precepts (five or eight).

Mahâyâna

Around the first century B.C.E., a new literature began to appear that introduced different perspectives and insights into the Buddha's teachings: Mahâyâna, "Great(er) Vehicle" or "Career," as opposed to the earlier, monastically and scholastically oriented schools referred to above. Among the differences in attitude between

Theravâda, the sole surviving school of the Individual Vehicle, and Mahâyâna, as perceived by the Mahâyâna teachers, are the following:

1. A new path was introduced, that of the Bodhisattva (a being who strove for awakening or Buddhahood). Instead of pursuing *Nirvâna*, which resulted in the total removal of the enlightened being from the world of suffering, Bodhisattvas vowed to continue to devote themselves to ensuring the salvation of all living beings in the world of suffering. As a result, the ideal individual of Theravâda Buddhism, the Arhant [AR-hunt] (one who has achieved *Nirvâna*) was rejected and replaced by the ideal individual in Mahâyâna, the Bodhisattva. Certain implications arise from this shift in teaching:

    a. The emphasis is on saving others, not just oneself.

    b. Saving others requires methods and conduct that are certain to cause the unenlightened to see the light. This is known as "Skillful Means."

    c. All beings have the potential to become Buddhas. This reflected the basic Buddhist teaching that the Buddha was a Bodhisattva prior to his enlightenment at age 35. In the Theravâda tradition, however, only one Buddha is recognized in this present world age—Gautama—and only one present Bodhisattva currently exists, Maitreya. He is expected to emerge many thousands or even millions of years from now as a Buddha. Contrary to this view is the Mahâyânist view that Buddhahood is open to all because all beings possess Buddha Nature.

    d. More emphasis is placed on the practice of compassion (i.e., wisdom put to practice).

2. New, divine-like Buddhas and Bodhisattvas were introduced into the literature. Among the Bodhisattvas who are especially important are

    *   Avalokiteshvara (in China, known as Kuan-yin or Guanyin; in Japan, Kwannon), the Bodhisattva of Compassion;

    *   Mâñjushrî (China, Wen-shu; Japan, Mon-ju), the Bodhisattva of Wisdom;

    *   Kshitigarbha (China, Ti-tsang), the Bodhisattva who saves the dead from hell and who (as Jizô in Japan) watches over the welfare of children, pregnant women, and travelers;

    *   Samantabhadra (China, P'u-hsien; Japan, Fugen), the Bodhisattva who represents universal kindness; and

    *   Maitreya (China, Mi-lo-fo; Japan, Mi-roku), the future Buddha who in China is often wrongly identified as the Laughing Buddha (see "Common Misunderstandings and Stereotypes" below).

Among the Buddhas of note are

- Amitâbha (China, A-mi-to; Japan, Amida), the most popular of Buddhas who resides over the Western Paradise;

- Bhaishajyaguru (China, Yao-shih-liu-li-kuang-wang-ju-lai) or the Medicine Buddha, who is popular in China as the curer of all diseases;

- Vairocana (China, P'a-lu-che-na; Japan, Dai-nichi), the Sunlike Buddha;

- Ratnasambhava (China, Bao-sheng-fo; Japan, Hosho), the Buddha of the South;

- Akshobhya (China, A-ch'u; Japan, Ashuku), the Buddha of the East; and

- Amoghasiddhi (China, Ch'eng-chiu fu; Japan, Fuku jo-ju), the Buddha of the North.

Vajrayâna

In Tibet and Nepal around 500 C.E., the third type of Buddhism appeared with the introduction of new sacred books known as *tantras*. This tradition, called today Vajrayâna, the "Diamond" or "Apocalyptic" Vehicle, which spread to Mongolia, parts of China, Bhutan, Sikkim, Ladakh, and parts of Russia among the Buriat Mongols and Kalmucks, emphasized ritual and magical means of achieving Buddhahood. The tradition was philosophically based on the Mahâyâna teachings but placed emphasis on technical, magical, and ritual means that were radically different from earlier practices to accelerate enlightenment. More specifically, *mantras* (sacred language); *mudrâs* (hand gestures); *mandalas* (symbolic models of the cosmos); special deities; and instruments such as the bell, ritual dagger, hand drum, and scepter are employed to this end.

Common Misunderstandings and Stereotypes

It is important to keep in mind that sweeping statements about Buddhist behavior and belief cannot be made. For instance, not all Buddhists meditate (some schools do not advocate it); not all Buddhists are vegetarians (this is especially true of Japanese Buddhists); not all Buddhist monks and nuns are celibate; and not all Buddhists hold to the teaching of nonviolence.

Furthermore, there is no general ethical system or rigid ethical code for Buddhists except perhaps for the Five Precepts (not to kill, steal, lie; not to abuse speech or sex). Opinions about the rightness or wrongness of a specific action will often depend on one's national background or specific circumstances. Opinions differ on such important issues as warfare, abortion, and homosexuality. In general, however, the rule of thumb for Buddhists is that if an action is harmful to oneself or to others, it must be avoided. The problem that often arises in real-life situations, though, is that what is harmful to one may be helpful to another. The decision as to whether such an action is to be avoided or permitted will be open to debate among Buddhists.

"Buddhists worship statues of Shâkyamuni (Buddhism's founder) and other Buddhas."
Statues of Buddhas and Bodhisattvas do not constitute a form of worship in the Western sense. Although descriptions and Buddhist literature might give the impressions that these beings are divinities, they are not in the strict sense. They are not necessarily worshipped as gods, although it is quite possible for less sophisticated Buddhists to view the Buddhas and Bodhisattvas as gods or emanations of God.

"The Buddha is a fat, jolly figure who doesn't seem very religious."
What is known as the Laughing Buddha—a fat, disheveled, figure standing with raised hands or sitting with a laughing visage found in gift shops and restaurants—is actually Maitreya, or more accurately, the Chinese monk Pu-tai (Hotei in Japan), who was posthumously connected to Maitreya in the eleventh century. Pu-tai (Hemp Bag, Glutton) was known for his hemp bag containing all sorts of oddities that was the continual object of curiosity, especially of children. In Ch'an, or Zen Buddhism, he represents a class of individuals who pose as religious eccentrics.

Classroom Concerns

Because of the general ignorance about Buddhist teaching and practice in the United States, some students might view it as a cult. It is important to explain its key ideas and its moral code as worthy of careful study and discussion.

It is also important to be aware that the different calendars employed by Buddhists of different traditions and nationalities—especially regarding the Buddha's birthday and New Year's celebrations—can be confusing. If you have Buddhist students in class, consult them or their parents about when they celebrate these events. (See Appendix B for a calendar.)

Population Data

It is very difficult to determine an accurate number of Buddhists. Numbers range from 250 million to 500 million worldwide, with the *World Almanac and Book of Facts*[9] citing 340 million. Buddhist countries include Sri Lanka, Thailand, Vietnam, Cambodia, Myanmar (Burma), Laos, China, Taiwan, Korea, Japan, Tibet, Mongolia, Nepal, Sikkim, and Bhutan (now under Indian control). The estimate of the number of Buddhists in the United States, more specifically, in the Buddhist Churches of America, is 230,000. Based on the number of immigrants from predominantly Buddhist countries, this number is probably closer to 500,000.

—J.S.

Notes

1. Quoted from A. K. Warder, reviser of 2d ed., *The Anguttara-Nikāya,* vol. 1. Rev. Richard Morris, ed. (London: Luzac for the Pali Text Society, 1961).

2. The term *Hînayâna* (Lesser Vehicle) is considered a derogatory term by those within this tradition. Therefore, Theravâda will replace it.

3. The expression is taken from Marylin M. Rhie and Robert A. F. Thurman, *Wisdom and Compassion: The Sacred Act of Tibet* (New York: Harry N. Abrams, 1991), 15.

4. Ibid.

5. An offshoot of the Nichiren School is Soka Gakkai, which aggressively seeks converts and has attained a modest following among young professionals in the United States and Great Britain.

6. All other schools belonging to the Individual Vehicle, of which the traditional number was established to be 18 (including the Theravâda) as early as 300 years after the death of the Buddha, have long since disappeared.

7. The Metta Forest Monastery in Valley Center, Calif., is an example of a forest hermitage. The monk in charge is Thanissaro Bhikku.

8. The precepts are the refraining from (1) taking life, (2) stealing, (3) sexual misconduct, (4) lying, (5) drinking alcohol, (6) eating after noontime, (7) watching dancing, singing, and shows, (8) adorning oneself with garlands, perfumes, and ointments, (9) using a high bed, and (10) receiving gold and silver.

9. Robert Famighetti, ed. *World Almanac and Book of Facts* (New York: World Almanac Books/Funk & Wagnalls, 1997), 646.

Further Reading

Snelling, John. *Buddhism in Russia: The Story of Agvan Dorzhiev, Lhasa's Emissary to the Tsars.* Rockport, ME: Element Books, 1993.

Snelling, John. *The Elements of Buddhism.* Longmead, Shaftesbury, Dorset, UK: Element Books, 1990.

Chinese Religions: An Overview

Unlike the religions rooted in the Near East (Judaism, Christianity, Islam, and Baha'i), which retain their individuality and uniqueness, China has combined its three major religions—Confucianism, Taoism, and Buddhism—into one synthetic whole. Add to this mix Chinese folk religion, which resembles Buddhism and Taoism, and the general observation is that Chinese religions are an amorphous mass assimilated by the Chinese public. One might assert that all Chinese are socially Confucian and individually Taoist at the same time. These two native religions influenced Buddhism in China in such a way that it is markedly different from the Buddhism practiced in South and Southeast Asia. China thus reflects a very different response to the multiplicity of religious traditions found in the West—a response based on accommodation and syncretism (religious mixing) rather than exclusion and isolation.

Some generalizations about Chinese philosophy, religion, and tradition might help to bring order to what non-Chinese might consider a chaotic and incomprehensible mix of separate traditions:

1. Chinese religions and traditions are relatively practical in approach to the affairs of the living. They are more centered on the concerns of the individual in this world of the living and less concerned with the metaphysical or the spiritual world, which is considered to be beyond the world of the living. Generally speaking, the state is more important than religious establishments, and humanistic concerns take precedence over divine concerns or speculation. A creator god, for instance, is simply not discussed to any great extent, nor is such a being considered important enough to affect one's way of life.

This chapter is intended to explain the unique mix of religions in Chinese history. For practical data on Buddhism, Confucianism, and Taoism as they relate to the classroom, see the separate chapters on these traditions.

2. Chinese religious activity centers around a wisdom that orientates individuals to living a fulfilled and harmonious life here and now.

3. The achievement of a fulfilled and harmonious life is discussed and practiced in Confucianism, Taoism, Buddhism, and folk religion. All follow a *Tao* [dow] (Way) that leads one to the fulfilled life, but their respective ways of achieving this goal are fundamentally different.

Confucianism

Confucianism, or the Way of Confucius, is essentially moralistic or ethical in tone, emphasizing tradition, human relationships, rituals, and reason. The ultimate purpose was to construct a society that exemplified the *Tao*. In the sense that Confucianism emphasizes tradition, it has preserved those practices and viewpoints that, over the centuries, help to define what it means to be Chinese. For example, ancestor worship has a history of practice that goes back at least 3,500 years. Furthermore, acceptance of a supreme being or purposeful force (Heaven) that regulates the cosmic order has been and is part of Confucianism, as was the role of the Emperor as Son of Heaven who controlled the human order. As envisioned today, Confucianism is more a way of life or philosophy than a religion, for it is a systematic and reflective deliberation on living in this world. Confucian temples do exist, but they are not equivalent to the churches, synagogues, or temples of other religions. They were built with the intention of providing a place to honor Confucius, not to worship the gods. His birthday is commemorated September 28 at Taipei's Confucian Temple. Befitting Confucius as the greatest of Chinese teachers, this day is also Teachers' Day in the Republic of China.

Taoism

Taoism, on the whole, is opposed to the Confucian perspective. The *Tao*, as understood in Confucianism by the Taoists, had been perverted by reason and society. The *Tao* instead was to be found in nature. This perspective, therefore, emphasizes not the intellectual and moral side of humanity but rather the emotional. Whereas Confucianism emphasizes social living and obligations, Taoism emphasizes the presocial individual; whereas conformity is expected in Confucianism, dissent and free will are emphasized in Taoism. It is not uncommon, therefore, for one to picture the artist, poet, and hermit as Taoists, or to associate the esoteric and bizarre as more closely associated with Taoism.

Unlike Confucianism, Taoism is more than a philosophy. In fact, the roots of Taoism appear in early Chinese history with the practice of shamanism and all that it entails (see the chapter "Taoism"). During the fifth or sixth century B.C.E. and later, philosophical Taoism appeared, beginning with Lao Tzu's book, *The Way and Its Power*. This was followed by the more speculative thinking in the book *Chuang Tzu* (presumably by the author of the same name), which led to later expressions in literature, painting, and reclusive behavior.

Later still, probably around the second century C.E., came an increasing concern for the attainment of immortality by various practices and the concoction and drinking of elixirs. The alchemical side of Taoism in attaining transcendence of the limitations of life through breath control, sexual hygiene, dietary regimens, and elixirs became common. Also, the establishment of a religious Taoism, with the inclusion of a pantheon of various entities (nature gods, folk heroes, sages, and generals) originated at about the same time.

Buddhism

Buddhism, although a non-Chinese religion, adjusted to Chinese culture in the centuries following its introduction into China in the first century C.E. (or the second century B.C.E., according to some traditions). Unlike Taoism, however, which taught that life was valuable and should be enjoyed, Buddhism viewed all life as suffering. If Taoism was life-affirming, Buddhism sought to transcend life in this world. The crossbreeding of Buddhist, Confucian, and Taoist teachings occurred in the third and fourth centuries through the Chinese intelligentsia familiar with the literature of the three traditions. Taoism especially was believed to be similar to the Buddhist philosophy and certain Buddhist practices, mostly due to influences brought to bear on Buddhism by Taoism and vice-versa. For instance, Taoist terms were employed by scholars to translate Buddhist concepts into Chinese. This was called *ko-i* Buddhism, the use of the Taoist terminology of Lao Tzu to interpret Buddhist concepts. Taoism in turn was influenced by Buddhism perceiving itself as possessing a systematic body of doctrines contained within a literature, a concept that was adopted by Taoism. The making of statues also was taken over from the Buddhists. Even the biography of Lao Tzu was based on that of the Buddha. Some people even claim that Lao Tzu traveled to India and was none other than the Buddha. Also, the Neo-Taoist teaching of the Mystery (fourth to sixth century C.E.), involving the notion of being empty and nothing, appealed to some Buddhist scholars because of its similarity to the Buddhist emphasis on liberating oneself from all excessive and wrong desires.

Confucian differences with Buddhism lay in the Buddhist emphasis on the spiritual and its refusal to venerate the king or emperor (such veneration was a fundamental trait of state Confucianism). Yet, a poet in the fourth century C.E. suggested that Confucius and Buddha were simply teaching from differing points of view: the outside (the Confucian emphasis on corruption in society) and the inside (the Buddhist stress on underlying truth). The eventual outcome in China was accommodation of both of these philosophies. By 500 C.E., Buddhist rites were practiced; Buddhist monasteries and temples proliferated; Buddhist monks and nuns were numerous and respected. Taoism borrowed from Buddhism; Confucian families, especially women, embraced Buddhism.

Part of the success of Buddhism in China was because of the translating activities of Chinese and non-Chinese scholars over the centuries, resulting in the eventual dissemination of popular teachings. Among the teachings in the more popular and devotional Mahâyâna Buddhist tradition (see the chapter "Buddhism") were those of the celestial Bodhisattvas (figures who delayed their entry into full *Nirvâna*, or bliss, so as to help others achieve it) and the Pure Land doctrine. Regarding the latter, one strove to be reborn in the Pure Land (paradise) to achieve with greater facility final liberation.

Folk Religion

Folk religion is mainly part and parcel of a number of secular and social institutions. Consisting of numerous gods and goddesses, the folk religion emphasizes the establishment of relationships with these divine beings. Although similar to Taoism in this category, many of the divinities in folk religion are not included in Taoism. Like Buddhism, salvation in Chinese folk religion is open to all who follow the religion. In Taiwan (the Republic of China), the divinities that are of particular importance are the God of Heaven, who is associated with order and justice; the Earth God, to whom numerous temples are dedicated; and the House God, who receives offerings when the family moves into a new home. Other popular divinities include the patron goddess of fishermen, Matsu, as well as a number of divinities who were originally human; the healer Hua T'uo, who lived sometime between the first and third centuries C.E.; and the warrior Kuan Yu, who lived during the period of the Three Kingdoms (221–280 C.E.). Also part of the folk religion are the Wang Yeh of Taiwan, celestial spirits who protect humanity against evil spirits and from epidemics. Some Chinese (mostly of *Hakka* descent) also worship the Three Kings of the Mountains.

In addition to worship of these divinities, geomancy (a form of divination involving lines and figures) and physiognomy (divination based on facial features or judging human character based on facial features) are practiced.

—*J.S.*

Further Reading

Allison, Robert E. ed. *Understanding the Chinese Mind: The Philosophical Roots.* Hong Kong: Oxford University Press, 1989.

Ch'en, Kenneth. *Buddhism in China.* Princeton, NJ: Princeton University Press, 1964.

de Bary, Wm. Theodore, Wing-Tsit Chan, and Burton Watson, comps. *Sources of Chinese Tradition.* Vol. 1. New York and London: Columbia University Press, 1960.

Eliade, Mircea, ed. "Taoism," *The Encyclopedia of Religion.* Vol. 14. New York: Macmillan, 1987, pp. 288–317.

The Texts of Taoism: Part I (The Tao Te Ching of Lao Tzu; The Writings of Chuang Tzu) (Books I–XVII); Part II (The Writings of Chuang Tzu) (Books XVIII–XXXIII); The T'ai Shang Tractate of Actions and Their Retributions; Appendices I–VIII (Part II). New York: Dover Publications, 1962 [reprint of the 1891 edition, published in the Sacred Books of the East Series, Volumes 39 and 40].

Watson, Burton, trans. *The Complete Works of Chuang Tzu.* New York: Columbia University Press, 1968.

The bust of Confucius/Master K'ung is the traditional symbol of Confucianism.

Chinese Religions
Confucianism

Origins

The origins of Confucianism occur in the sixth and fifth centuries B.C.E. in the person of Confucius (*K'ung Fu Tzu*, or "Master K'ung": 551–479 B.C.E.). Born to a soldier father, he might have been an illegitimate child but nevertheless belonged to the aristocracy. He was educated, trained in archery and music, and held minor offices as a young man, though he never succeeded in the political realm. Confucius was concerned with the burning issue of the day—the protracted decline of the social order that started in the eighth century B.C.E. and led to a long period of civil strife that was not to end until the third century B.C.E. In such an age of decadence and warfare, the overriding issue of the time among philosophers was how to restore the social order and overcome the instability rampant in China.

Confucius was born in the state of Lu, which considered itself the custodian of Chou culture. (The Chou dynasty ruled China from 1122 to 256 B.C.E. but had only nominal control from the eighth century B.C.E. on). His solution to the turmoil of his time was to return to the ancient traditions and practices established in the early days of the dynasty that were now being neglected. Taken in this context, Confucius did not consider himself an innovator but rather a transmitter of the teachings of the ancients.

19

Beliefs

What we have left of Confucius' teachings are a series of brief sayings and observations recorded in the *Analects*. His role was, therefore, to preserve the social order and its ideals encompassed in the traditional civilization. This took on definitive form during the Chou dynasty. He did so by shaping the moral habits of its leaders and, by the example of the leaders, their subjects. The essence of his teaching was to provide a system of right conduct that operated on three planes: individual, social, and political. The outcome of right conduct resulted in the building of individual character, the discharging of social obligations, and the administering of moral government.

In the Chinese context, the standard of conduct, the *Tao* (Way), was an ideal way of life for both the individual and the state. The individual who strove to reach this standard was known as the Gentleman, or person of noble character, and the individual who actually accomplished the goal of putting the *Tao* into practice was known as the Sage.

The specific virtues and values that underlay the three planes were:

1. *li* [lee]—conduct: The rules of conduct and responsibility that governed all human modes of civilized relationship, including one's relations with parents during their lifetime (filiality) and after their death (ancestral worship), and with superiors, from simple rules of etiquette to formal court ritual.

2. *jen* [ruhn]—benevolence, affection, or humanity: The performance of actions that manifest what we might perceive as humanity or humaneness. The written Chinese character for *jen* signifies "two" and "man," suggesting the basis of humanity and human relationships.

3. *yi* [yee]—the sense of rightness or appropriateness of action.

The three virtues are interrelated. For instance, *jen* must conform to what is right (*yi*); *yi*, which is performed with the spirit of humanity (*jen*), is executed through conduct (*li*). Other virtues are also mentioned by Confucius. For instance, in *Analects* 17:6, he observes that courtesy, generosity, honesty, persistence, and kindness comprise *jen*. It is clear, therefore, that Confucius emphasized the human sphere, not the divine; this present life and not the future life; moral action based on traditional customs and not ritual or ceremonial action for the sake of empty convention.

Developments did occur after his death. For one, the divine sphere became increasingly important, with the Emperor, as the Son of Heaven, responsible for the proper functioning of the social and natural order through ritual action and retaining the Mandate of Heaven (divine or providential blessings). Confucianism under the Han dynasty (206 B.C.E.–220 C.E.) became the state ideology. The Confucianist emphasis on the bureaucracy, the family system, the civil service examination system, and study of the Five Classics were paramount. These and later developments help to define the Confucianist way of life. As a way of life, as an ethic, and in some aspects as a religion (such as ritual and myth), Confucianism helps to define the Chinese character in much the same way that the so-called Civil Religion of the United States helps to define the American character, or Hinduism the Indian character.

The following observations can be made about Confucianism:

1. Confucianism is regarded more as a philosophy, a way of life, and a scholarly tradition than a religion, but with a political or royal ideology that included the ritual duty of the Emperor.

2. The inner life of the Confucian is governed by such virtues as humanity and rightness.

3. The outer expression of the Confucian is manifested by the rules of conduct that govern an individual's life and that are primarily but not exclusively encompassed in filial piety and ancestral worship. Filial piety, which was expanded in the Doctrine of the Mean (see "Sacred Books/Scriptures" below) to include the fivefold relationship between minister and ruler, son and father, wife and husband, younger and elder brother, and friends, is considered the foundation of virtue and the root of civilization. In other words, the family is the foundation of society.

4. Confucianists (and Chinese culture in general) place great stress on education. As early as the Han dynasty, mastering the Five Classics was the means of entering civil service and served as the basis of the state cult. Education was viewed as the primary mean to success.

5. The Doctrine of the Mean stresses that human nature should be in harmony with the larger universe. It states:

    > What Heaven [the early Chou dynasty name for the Supreme
    > Being who watched over the conduct of humans and the laws
    > of nature] imparts to man is called human nature. To follow our
    > nature is called the Way. Cultivating the Way is called education.

    The emphasis on achieving harmony with Heaven's will or mandate becomes the basis of political philosophy in the role of the Emperor and in the role of the Gentleman.

6. The Confucian strives to achieve harmony in personal conduct and convictions. In other words, one must be in harmony with one's nature as well as with the dictates of Heaven.

7. Connected to the role and goal of harmony was the early (third century B.C.E.) inclusion of the *yin-yang* (literally, "shady (yin) and sunny (yang) side of the hill") the concept of dual powers that permeate the universe: female and male, cold and heat, darkness and light, passivity and aggression, rest and activity, withdrawal and expansion. Maintaining harmony

of the twofold nature of reality was to be of supreme importance to the Emperor in the performance of rituals. It also took on importance in other areas outside the specific philosophical range of Confucianism, such as medicine.

In conclusion, the Confucianism of Confucius was primarily concerned with the human sphere, especially moral conduct that derived its worth from its association with Heaven's will. Later, more emphasis was placed on the workings of the cosmos and its relationship with the human sphere. In so doing, Confucianism adopted teachings from non-Confucian philosophies and practices. This sharing of teachings with other major philosophies, Taoism included, has led the Chinese to take a non-exclusive view of their religious life. Confucianists—whether Chinese, Korean, or Japanese—may also profess to practice elements identified with Taoism, Buddhism, Shintoism,[1] or Christianity without denying the Confucian orientation that exists within their culture.

Sacred Books/Scriptures

Writings especially prestigious to Confucians in particular and Chinese in general are the Five Classics and Four Books. The Five Classics are the *Book of History* (which includes the reports and speeches of early Chou rulers), the *Book of Odes* (about 300 poems from early Chou times), the *Classic on Changes* (a book on divination), the *Classic on Ritual* (three texts, of which the most famous is the Book of Rites), and the *Spring and Autumn Annals*, an account of Lu (the Chinese state) from 722 to 481 B.C.E.

The Four Books are the *Analects* of Confucius, the *Doctrine of the Mean* (which describes the duties of the Gentleman, social obligations, and the virtues of moderation and balance), the *Great Learning*, and the *Book of Mencius* (Mencius [371–288 B.C.E.] was the second greatest Confucian philosopher).

Practices

Practices performed by the populace (and not the formal state ceremonies that were once performed in China and Korea) include those involving four important life-cycle rituals: birth, maturity, marriage, and death.

Ceremonies surrounding the birth include the protection of the mother-to-be by the Spirit of the Fetus (*T'ai-shen*), the disposal of the placenta, the mother resting for a month and being given a special diet, and the baby being supplied with all necessary items on the anniversaries celebrated in the first, fourth, and twelfth months.

The ceremony of reaching maturity is rarely celebrated today. When performed, the young adult is served chicken at a gathering celebrating the event.

The marriage customs involve the proposal, the engagement, the dowry (which is carried to the groom's home in a procession), the giving of gifts to the bride (generally equal to the dowry), the visit of the groom to the bride's home, the groom taking the bride to his home, the marriage and reception, and the bride's serving breakfast to the groom's parents the morning after the marriage.

The ceremonies surrounding death involve a number of actions required of the family. The body is washed, dressed, and placed in a coffin. Usually a Taoist or Buddhist officiant performs the ritual. Liturgies are held on the seventh, ninth, and 49th days after the burial and on the first and third anniversaries of the deceased.

Ancestral worship, which involves an elaborate set of practices, is performed each year. One practice includes a number of events taking place over a 15-day period, among which are the preparation of the family shrine, where offerings and homage are made; and the hiring of priests (if the family can afford them) to announce the dead to deities, read scriptures to help in the ancestors' proceeding to the Western Heaven of Happiness, and perform the "burning of the bags" (*shu pao*) ceremony for the ancestors (bags containing silver ingots bear the name of the male ancestor and his wife).

Main Subgroups

Since Confucianism is not a religion in the same sense as Christianity or Buddhism, there is no orthodox Confucian church nor are there sects. It is primarily the cultural and traditional sides of society with inclusion of significant rituals (such as ancestral rites) that provide its defining characteristics.

Perhaps the best way to view Confucianism is through an historical perspective. From the teachings of Confucius developed the state ideology of the Han dynasty that not only included the Confucian (i.e., Confucius and later philosophers such as Mencius and Hsün Tzu) teachings of human behavior, nature, society, and government but also cosmological teachings and divination practices that were not originally Confucian. Neo-Confucianism emerged much later during the Sung dynasty (960–1279 C.E.) with its emphasis on a metaphysical approach to understanding human nature and the human condition.

Some people view the Confucianism of Japan and Korea to be separate schools. This is especially true for the Confucianism of Japan because of the profound influence of Neo-Confucianism in Tokugawa era Japan (1603–1867). Japanese business practices today reflect the influence of Confucianism, such as the notion of lifetime employment by Japanese companies and the paternalistic relationship between superior and subordinate.

Common Misunderstandings and Stereotypes

While Confucianism itself may not be well known in the United States, it should be noted that the East Asian cultures have all been significantly influenced by the Confucian ethic. It is typically understood to be a philosophy with political, social, ethical, and somewhat metaphysical overtones coupled with ritual and ceremonial practices. In popular culture, sometimes-humorous remarks beginning with "Confucius say. . ." often take on negative racial overtones that demean the Chinese and their culture. Furthermore, the strong emphasis on education in Chinese culture sometimes leads to the misguided impression that the Chinese (and Asians in general) are genetically predisposed to general intellectual and mathematical skills.

Classroom Concerns

It is suggested that teachers emphasize at opportune times (e.g., the Chinese New Year), or along with the study of Chinese history or religions, the significant contributions to civilization made by the Chinese. Contributions include numerous inventions (printing, paper, and explosives, to name but a few); the Great Wall of China; and the importance of the family, elders, education, and literacy in Chinese culture.

Population Data

The number of Confucians worldwide is estimated to be about 55,254,000 according to the *World Almanac and Book of Facts*.[2] The majority reside in China and Korea, with small numbers on the other continents. North America has only 26,000 Confucians. Confucian values, however, permeate Chinese, Korean, Vietnamese, and other regions where there is Chinese influence—Taoism, Chinese folk religion, and Buddhism.

—*J.S.*

Notes

1. Shintoism/Shinto is the native religion of Japan that stresses the presence of divine powers, *kami* [KAH-mee], in nature (e.g., Mount Fujiyama). Shinto is not covered in this book because there are few practitioners in the United States.

2. Robert Famighetti, ed. *World Almanac and Book of Facts* (New York: World Almanac Books/Funk & Wagnalls, 1997), 646.

The yin-yang symbol indicates how such opposites as dark (yin) and light (yang), passive and active, winter and summer, and female and male interact and complement each other.

Chinese Religions
Taoism

Origins

Unlike other religious traditions, Taoism [DOW-ism] has neither a single origin (like Christianity or Islam) nor an indistinct origin (like Hinduism). There are rather two distinct sources for what we know today as Taoism: (1) the philosophers of the Warring States (civil war) period (403–221 B.C.E.) who followed a *Tao* (Way) of nature rather than a *Tao* of society, and (2) the shamans and magicians who, since the Shang dynasty (1523–1027 B.C.E.) and perhaps earlier, played an important role in the life of the ordinary Chinese population. Further developments in philosophical Taoism and shamanic (or popular) Taoism resulted in what is known as religious Taoism.

Philosophical Taoism

The earliest of the philosophers associated with the Taoist thought was Lao Tzu [LAOW-dzuh], who lived either in the sixth century B.C.E. or, according to some Western scholars, during the Warring States period, sometime during the fourth or third century B.C.E. Little is known of his life, and there is much discussion whether the legendary Lao Tzu was confused with an historical personage actually responsible for writing the *Tao Te Ching* [dow-duh-JING], namely Li Erh. It may be also that the *Tao Te Ching* of Lao Tzu was not the product of one person but actually a compilation of sayings by several teachers, all assuming the name Lao Tzu.

25

The second great philosopher of the Warring States period was Chuang Tzu [JWAHNG-dzuh] (369–286 B.C.E.), whose book of the same name reflects the teaching of the *Tao Te Ching* but is more mystical and intuitive and is somewhat more complex in its outlook.

Popular Taoism

The other root of Taoism lay in the activities of shamans [SHAW-muns] and magicians. Shamans are religious persons found worldwide who exhibit a number of unusual traits: magical flight, that is, communicating with spirits by traveling to their abode; magical healing by serving as mediators between spirits and humans; and the ability to enter into trance states for the purpose of journeying to the spirit world. Shamans in China typically were associated with the expulsion of evil spirits through magical healing, and engaged in magical flights to heavenly and demonic regions. Furthermore, they used dancing, juggling, and tricks to induce the descent of the spirits. Chinese shamans were known either as *wu* (wizard, witch, magic; dancing) or *fang-shih* (magician or scholar of magical recipes). Both men and women were shamans, with perhaps women being the more numerous. Female shamans were explicitly directed to exorcise the spirits at certain times of the year; to dance in times of drought or to perform certain gestures to encourage rain; to heal; and, in times of trouble, to entreat the spirits and engage in wailing and chanting. The association of women is significant because the Taoist ideal society is connected with matriarchal memories, femininity, and, later, emphasis on sexual techniques. For instance, female *wu* represented the *yin* (female, water) element in nature when rain rituals were enacted.

Religious Taoism

Besides the philosophical Taoism engendered by Lao Tzu and Chuang Tzu, a number of developments occurred over the centuries that became subsumed under what is generally known as religious Taoism. The connection between the philosophical and religious was maintained, however, in the primary objectives of Taoism: longevity, vitality, and a harmonious life. The regimen that took hold in religious Taoism included such techniques as alchemy, breath control and hygiene, magic, elixirs, and sexual techniques not unlike those of Buddhist Apocalyptic (Vajrayâna) Buddhism.

Although the ultimate origins of Taoism as a religion are partly located in the ancient tradition and context of shamanism, the more immediate origins occur during the first century B.C.E. Originating during this period was a popular movement dedicated to the culture hero Huang Ti (the legendary Yellow Emperor) and Lao Tzu. Known as the Huang-Lao philosophy, this movement divinized Lao Tzu and raised to prominence the practices mentioned above as well as those of astrology and divination. Many deities, including the divinized Lao Tzu, were also introduced. This movement was formally organized by the religious leader Chang Tao Ling in the second century C.E. As the first to be given the title of Heavenly

Teacher, a hereditary title that persists to the twentieth century with the Chang family, Chang Lao Ling is regarded as the historical founder of the Taoist religion.

Beliefs

The philosophy of Taoism in the *Tao Te Ching*, which is regarded as a political treatise for the ruler, may be summarized as follows:

1. The *Tao Te Ching* is a vision of reality or the order of nature known as the *Tao* (Way).

2. The *Tao* is regarded as an infinite whole that cannot be measured by human standards. Scattered throughout the *Tao Te Ching* are descriptions of the *Tao* as being empty, invisible, formless yet complete, eternal, and existing prior to heaven and earth. The *Tao* is spontaneous, simple, and natural.

3. The highest embodiment of *Tao* is *Te* [dŭ] (Power—the internalized *Tao*); it is the *Tao* dwelling in objects causing them to be what they are, a concept that resembles the notion of potentiality.

4. As the embodiment of *Tao*, *Te* embodies effortlessness and spontaneity. Thus, the highest *Te* is non-action (*wu-wei*).

5. The Taoist philosophy is a corrective to excessive deliberation, excessive activity, excessive passion, and artificiality—in short, a corrective to the increasing complexity of living.

6. The solution in life is to return to the *Tao*, to conform to the *Tao*, to move like the *Tao*. In other words, the solution is to return to simplicity, to plainness, to a state of infancy, and to the practice of non-action (i.e., to perform a minimum of action); and to become more natural or to follow nature.

7. The suggestion in the *Tao Te Ching* is to correct the imbalance that has arisen in the world. Thus the theme of the *Tao Te Ching* is to loosen one's hold on the conventional, the socially acceptable, and the so-called normal and "keep to the center." Scattered throughout the text are admonitions to adhere to the feminine rather than the masculine, the passive rather than the active, non-desire rather than desire, unselfishness rather than selfishness, and so on.

Incorporated in Taoist philosophy were the complementary principles of *yin* and *yang*. Although not unique to Taoism, they were employed in the *Tao Te Ching* as the harmonious duality in the cosmos. The complementary natures of sun and shade, heat and cold, and summer and winter are examples of *yin* and *yang* operating in nature. Humans, men and women, have both masculine and feminine principles within them, and maintenance of harmony between the masculine and feminine is essential to physical and mental health.

The second great book of philosophical Taoism, the *Chuang Tzu*, agrees in part with the *Tao Te Ching*. For instance, it regards the *Tao* as the indescribable equivalent of the natural or cosmic order, and it emphasizes the unity and spontaneity of nature. Furthermore, the *Te*, the virtue or power (natural ability) that makes us what we are, is the movement of the *Tao*. An underlying theme of the teaching in the *Chuang Tzu* is that all beings should follow their nature, for to follow nature is to follow *Tao*. Anything that is not natural—the artificial, the non-spontaneous— only leads to misery. Thus, the *Chuang Tzu* states: "Emptiness, stillness, limpidity, silence, inaction [are] the substance of the *Tao* and its *Te*."

One area of difference between the two books is that the *Tao Te Ching* is a political text concerned with the action and proper rule of the sage-king, whereas the *Chuang Tzu* is designed for the private individual.

Sacred Books/Scriptures

The two most important philosophical books in Taoism are the *Tao Te Ching* and the *Chuang Tzu*. Scholarship has determined that the writer Li Erh may actually be responsible for compiling the *Tao Te Ching* and that it was not the product of one person but rather a compilation of sayings by several teachers, all assuming the name Lao Tzu. The *Chuang Tzu* was most probably compiled in the third century C.E. by the commentator Kuo Hsiang.

Religious Taoism possesses a large number of sacred books that are specifically associated with the various Taoist movements or sects. Many of these books are not open to the public but are reserved for initiates or those judged ready to receive the teachings.

Practices

Practices designed to promote health and longevity include alchemical practices (see "Origins", above), breathing exercises, movement exercises designed to circulate the *ch'i* (vital breath) and meditation. Divination with the I Ching (The Classic on Changes), interpreted in a Taoist context, is also popular. Social Taoism resulted in the development of sects and religious communities that included priests and, later, monastic institutions and monks. The latter two developed from Buddhist influence. The presence of priests and monastic institutions resulted in the introduction of ritual practices to celebrate the birthdays of gods, to ward off misfortune, to attain or maintain peace and prosperity, to promote the successful building of a house, and to ordain priests.

Main Subgroups

Taoist religio-political communities date from the second century C.E. with the appearance of the T'ien-shih Tao ("Way of the Heavenly Masters") under its first and foremost Heavenly Master, Chang Tao-ling (also considered the founder of the Taoist religion), and the T'ai-ping Tao ("Way of the Great Peace").

1. The first and most prominent sect developed into a religious movement under the Heavenly Master that is still prominent in Taiwan. An important ingredient of the practice of the priests of the school is healing the sick with exorcism or faith healing.

2. The second sect, founded by Chang-chiao, was a dissident movement that was millenarian (oriented to a future golden age) in nature. Chang-chiao had the reputation of a great healer, but he is known for teaching that 184 C.E. was to be the beginning of a new era. His followers, Yellow Turbans, wore yellow turbans as a distinctive sign of the sect. The insurrection was, however, brutally overthrown.

3. Established in the fourth century was the Mao Shan (Mount Mao) sect. It reacted to the Buddhist monastic organizations by forming its own community that was designed to perform the Taoist practices of meditation and of external and internal alchemies, as well as mediumistic practices and communication with deities through visualization.

4. The Ling Pao (Marvelous Treasure) sect of the fifth century introduced the worship of the T'ien Tsun (Heavenly Worthies).

5. In the twelfth century, the Ch'üan-chen (Completely Real) sect was founded by Wang Che (1112–1170). It advocated the amalgamation of Taoism, Confucianism, and Buddhism. It emphasized meditation as the major practice to achieve the Taoist goals.

Today, the Ch'üan-chen and the Way of the Heavenly Masters still exist. Another group, from Taiwan, the I-kuan Tao (Great Dao), has recently made its appearance in California. This is an international movement that emphasizes more outreach to the general population.

Common Misunderstandings and Stereotypes

Because many people in the United States have never heard of Taoism, stereotypes are not common. However, those who are familiar with Taoism in some way might consider it magical or superstitious. Though magic is an element of popular Taoism, it certainly does not apply to the tradition as a whole.

Classroom Concerns

It is suggested that teachers emphasize at appropriate times (e.g., the Chinese New Year), or in connection with the study of Chinese history, the many contributions to civilization made by the Chinese (printing, paper, explosives, etc.), the Great Wall of China, and the importance of the family, elders, education, and literacy in Chinese culture. Teachers might also explain how the Taoist emphasis on living in accord with nature can be beneficial both to one's health and to the environment.

Population Data

There is no way to determine the actual number of Taoists. The *World Almanac and Book of Facts.*[1] lists the worldwide total of Chinese folk religionists (defined by the almanac as adherents to a combination of practices and beliefs such as those related to local deities, ancestor veneration, Confucian ethics, Taoism, universism, divination, and some Buddhist elements) to be 149,336,000 (of which 126,000 are in North America). In Taiwan, where Taoism is more visible, there are almost 4 million Taoists, with 8,292 temples and 31,950 priests serving the community.

The international headquarters of the Taoist movement known as the I-kuan Tao (Great Dao) was established at El Monte, California, in 1994 because (according to its founders) of political instability in Taiwan and the large Chinese immigrant population in the United States.

—J.S.

Notes

1.   Robert Famighetti, ed. *World Almanac and Book of Facts* (New York: World Almanac Books/Funk & Wagnalls, 1997), 646.

The cross symbolizes the Roman cross on which Jesus was crucified. The circle surrounding the cross is less common in the West and more often found in Orthodox Christianity, where it signifies eternity with God, the goal of the Christian life.

Christianity: Common Elements

Origins

Christianity (from *Christos*, the Greek term for "Messiah") began with the birth of Jesus of Nazareth/Jesus Christ and developed over the first 75 years of the first century C.E. into a religion distinct from Judaism. Jesus, after a period of preaching and healing, was arrested by Pontius Pilate, head of the Roman occupation government in Judea, on suspicion that he might lead a revolt against the Romans and on complaints from the Jewish High Priest and some of his associates, who objected to certain religious teachings of Jesus. Jesus was crucified by the Romans. After the crucifixion, Jesus' followers proclaimed that God had raised Jesus from the dead and that Jesus had appeared before some of them. The apostle Paul and other missionaries began spreading the teachings of Jesus to the non-Jewish population of the Greco-Roman world.

This chapter is intended to explain what is common to Christianity. For particular data on African American Christianity, Christian Science, Mormonism/Church of Jesus Christ of Latter-day Saints, Orthodox Christianity, Jehovah's Witnesses, Protestant Christianity, Roman Catholic Christianity, and Seventh-day Adventists as they relate to the classroom, see the separate chapters on these religions.

Beliefs

Christianity proclaims that Jesus is the Messiah, first spoken of in Judaism, and also God's son who redeemed or rescued humankind from its sinful condition. He possesses both a human and a divine nature, and in his divinity, he is one in his very essence with God the Father, the God of the Jewish people. In addition, the Holy Spirit (Ghost), mentioned in the Gospels (see "Sacred Books/Scriptures" below), is also considered a divine being coequal with God the Father and Jesus. The Christian Godhead is called the Trinity because there are three personal manifestations of the one God—Father, Son, and Holy Spirit. Christians believe that Jesus will return to earth at some future point to defeat the powers of evil completely and to judge the living and the dead. Those who are redeemed will live forever with God in heaven, and those who are not redeemed will be condemned to hell.

Sacred Books/Scriptures

Christians accept both the Old Testament (identical to the Hebrew Bible of Judaism) and the New Testament as the revealed word of God. The Old Testament has three major divisions: Law/Torah (Genesis, Exodus, Leviticus, Numbers, Deuteronomy); Prophets (Former Prophets: Joshua, Judges, 1–2 Samuel, 1–2 Kings; Latter Prophets: Isaiah, Jeremiah, Ezekiel; and the 12 minor prophets); and Writings (Psalms, Proverbs, Job, Song of Songs, Ruth, Lamentations, Ecclesiastes, Esther, Daniel, Ezra-Nehemiah, 1–2 Chronicles). The New Testament consists of 27 books: four Gospels (Matthew, Mark, Luke, and John), the account of Jesus' life and teachings; one historical book (Acts of the Apostles); one so-called apocalyptic writing (Book of Revelation), urging Christians suffering under Roman persecution to remain steadfast and describing the end of time and the afterlife; and 21 letters to churches, more than half of which are attributed to Paul.

Practices

The vast majority of Christians practice two rituals or sacraments, baptism (the entry rite) and the Lord's Supper/Holy Communion/Eucharist (the consuming of bread and wine, which represent the presence of Jesus Christ).

With the exception of the Seventh-day Adventists, Christians observe Sunday as the Sabbath, the day most worship services take place and workaday activities are avoided. Other principal holy days include:

> **Advent**. A four-week period of spiritual preparation for the coming (advent) of Jesus at Christmas. It begins on the Sunday nearest November 30.

> **Christmas**. A celebration of the birthday of Jesus Christ: December 25 for Roman Catholics and Protestants and January 7 for Orthodox Christians. Some Orthodox Christians in this country celebrate Christmas on December 25 as an accommodation to Catholic and Protestant practice.

Lent. A 40-day period of penitence in February and March in preparation for Easter. Roman Catholics and Protestants mark the start of Lent with Ash Wednesday.

Good Friday (called Holy Friday by Orthodox Christians). A commemoration of the day Jesus died by crucifixion that occurs two days before Easter. Many Christians attend services on the afternoon of Good Friday at about the time Jesus is thought to have died.

Easter Sunday. A celebration of the resurrection of Jesus. Its timing is based on a lunar calendar and varies from year to year. (See "Calendar of Religious Holidays," Appendix B.)

Ascension Day. A commemoration of Jesus' ascent into heaven to sit at the right hand of God the Father. Ceremony occurs 40 days after Easter.

Pentecost Sunday. A celebration marking the descent of the Holy Spirit upon Jesus' apostles after his ascension into heaven. Ceremony occurs on the seventh Sunday after Easter.

With the exception of Advent and Christmas, the dates of these holy days are determined by the lunar calendar and thus vary from year to year. Because Orthodox Christians use a different calendar, they observe Holy (Good) Friday, Easter, and Ascension Day on different dates than Roman Catholics and Protestants. (See "Calendar of Religious Holidays," Appendix B.)

Main Subgroups

(Eastern) Orthodox. This traditional form of Christianity originated in the Middle East and Eastern Europe and is organized along national lines (Greek Orthodox, Russian Orthodox, etc.).

Roman Catholic. This, the largest branch of Christianity, began in Rome under Peter, the first bishop there, and accepts the authority of his successors, the popes.

Protestant. This most recent branch of Christianity began in western Europe in the sixteenth century as a protest against perceived abuses in Roman Catholicism and now includes numerous subdivisions (Anglicans, Lutherans, Methodists, Presbyterians, etc.).

Common Misunderstandings and Stereotypes

Because of Christianity's cultural acceptance and because the chapters on Catholic, Orthodox, and Protestant Christianity discuss misunderstandings specific to each, only one issue will be considered here. The term *Christian* is often used by evangelical and fundamentalist Christians (see the chapter "Fundamentalism") to describe themselves (as in the expression "When I became a Christian . . ."). Evangelical and fundamentalist Christians (or "born-again" believers), like all people, have every right to identify themselves in whatever way they wish. Many feel that they were only nominally Christian before their born-again experience or that their previous religious commitment was not authentically Christian. However, they need to realize that the term *Christianity* is also a generic description for anyone who accepts some form of the religion in its Catholic, Orthodox, Protestant, or other expressions. In other words, people other than evangelical and fundamentalist Christians also have the right to call themselves Christians.

Classroom Concerns

In light of the cultural dominance of Christianity in the United States, there is the potential for teachers to assume that everyone in class is a Christian of some sort and to proceed accordingly. However, the 14 percent of children in the United States who are not Christian include several million whose parents are Jewish, Muslim, Buddhist, Hindu, or followers of other religions, or of no religion. Their beliefs and sensibilities must also be considered and respected.

However, because Christianity has played a decisive role in the founding and development of this country, a study of the history of the United States in incomplete without a study of Christianity.

Population Data

The recent exhaustive survey by Kosmin and Lachman[1] cited in the introduction indicates that about 86 percent of the United States population (215 million) is Christian. There are about 1.5 billion Christians in the world.

—B.H.

Notes

1. Barry A. Kosmin and Seymour P. Lachman, *One Nation Under God: Religion in Contemporary American Society* (New York: Harmony Books, 1993), 1–17.

Further Reading

Carmody, Denise L., and John T. Carmody. *Christianity: An Introduction.* 3rd ed. Belmont, CA: Wadsworth, 1995.

McGrath, Alister E. *An Introduction to Christianity.* Cambridge, MA: Blackwell, 1997.

Christianity

African American Christianity

Origins

African slaves were introduced to Christianity by southern clergy and by slave owners. However, Africans interpreted the faith in ways unique to them by emphasizing: (1) the Exodus experience of the Hebrew slaves who finally gained their freedom (as black slaves hoped to), and (2) a distinctively African tradition in worship services through the use of songs, drums, and emotional intensity (particularly in sermons). Furthermore, African American Christians saw themselves as restoring the church to its original purity.

In colonial times, many blacks belonged to the Methodist and Baptist denominations, which today are predominantly composed of whites. However, experiences such as that of black Methodist pastor Richard Allen, who was asked to move—in the middle of prayer—to the balcony of a Methodist church in Philadelphia in 1787, resulted in his founding the African Methodist Episcopal Church and the formation of other predominantly black churches in subsequent years.

Beliefs

There is little difference in the theology of African American churches as compared to their Protestant or Catholic counterparts. The Bible, however, is interpreted quite literally by most black Protestants, and the emotional aspects of worship are emphasized. In fact, the Pentecostal movement began in Los Angeles in 1906 under the leadership of African American minister William Seymour, who stressed speaking in tongues (believed by Pentecostals to be foreign languages of divine inspiration unknown to the speaker) as the final step in human sanctification. The so-called Holiness Churches also originated in the African American community with emphasis on the conversion experience as freeing one from sin and ensuring salvation.

Sacred Books/Scriptures

Black Christians accept the same Bible as other Christians.

Practices

There are no significant differences in such practices as baptism and the Lord's Supper/Holy Communion, or in the order of the worship service as compared to most mainly white Christian churches. There is, however, a different emotional tenor in black churches compared to white churches: more music (often with a rhythm and blues motif), more singing, more responsiveness on the part of congregants, more hand clapping, and other overt expressions of one's religious feelings.

A distinctively black holiday, though not religious as such, has a quasi-religious spirit: Kwanzaa [KWAHN-zuh] (Kiswahili for "first fruits of the harvest"), a seven-day celebration of African American values and traditions and their continued validity. Celebration occurs from December 26 to January 1, with a different virtue stressed each day: unity, self-determination, collective work and responsibility, cooperative economics, purpose, creativity, and faith. Day six is the highlight of the festival, with a communal feast, music, speeches, and the honoring of elders.

Main Subgroups

The largest black Protestant denomination is the National Baptist Convention, U.S.A., with 7.8 million members. It is followed in size by the African Methodist Episcopal Church (3.5 million), the Progressive National Baptist Convention (2.5 million), the African Methodist Episcopal Zion Church (1.2 million), and the Christian Methodist Episcopal Church (718,000). There are more than 2.5 million African American Catholics, and some blacks who belong to mainly white churches, particularly the Assemblies of God (Pentecostals) and Jehovah's Witnesses.

Common Misunderstandings and Stereotypes

There are many stereotypes about blacks that center around cultural rather than religious misunderstandings. However, there is some overlap in stereotypes:

"Blacks are lacking in moral discipline and self-control."
In fact, church-going African Americans tend to be quite strict with their children and very conservative on moral issues such as abortion, gay rights, and pornography.

"Black churches are hotbeds of political activity in violation of federal law regarding tax-exempt organizations."
Although it is true that African American churches have been a focal point for educational and organizational efforts to obtain civil rights, black preachers are not substitute precinct workers advising their congregants how to vote.

Classroom Concerns

It is important to recognize the distinctiveness of African American Christianity and its role in strengthening black culture and combating white racism over the past 300 years.

Both Kwanzaa and the birthday of Rev. Martin Luther King Jr. (January 15) are significant events for African Americans. On these days (as well as during February, Black History Month), teachers are encouraged to discuss contributions made by blacks to the history and culture of the United States.

Population Data

About 82 percent (24 million) of the 30 million African Americans in the United States are Protestant. About 9 percent of the black population in the United States is Catholic, and 1 percent is Muslim. Six percent indicated no religious affiliation; one percent belonged to other religions (especially Santeiria, an Afro-Cuban movement with a large following in the Miami area); one percent refused to answer the question on a recent survey.[1]

—B.H.

Notes

1. Barry A. Kosmin and Seymour P. Lachman, *One Nation Under God: Religion in Contemporary American Society* (New York: Harmony Books, 1993), 131, 141–42.

Further Reading

Lincoln, C. Eric, and Lawrence H. Mamiya. *The Black Church in the African American Experience*. Durham, NC: Duke University Press, 1990.

Paris, Peter. *The Social Teachings of the Black Churches*. Philadelphia: Fortress Press, 1985.

Roberts, James Deotis. *Black Theology Today: Liberation and Contextualization*. New York: Edwin Mellen Press, 1983.

Christianity

Christian Science/ Church of Christ, Scientist

Origins

The Church of Christ, Scientist was founded by Mrs. Mary Baker Eddy (1821–1910) in 1879 in Boston, Massachusetts. Mrs. Eddy wrote *Science and Health with Key to the Scriptures*, a textbook of spiritual healing and a key for understanding the Bible. She reorganized her Church in 1892 as The First Church of Christ, Scientist. There is only one Church of Christ, Scientist, which includes the Mother Church in Boston and its branches around the world. She began publishing an international newspaper, *The Christian Science Monitor*, in 1908.

Beliefs

God, who is Spirit, and his spiritual creation (which is an expression of God) constitutes the only reality, and believing in "matter" is a limited, temporal, and incorrect view of present reality. God and his creation are good; and sickness, sorrow, death, evil, and sin are not ordained or sustained by God. Christian Scientists make a distinction between "human beings," which is the worldly, material view, and "man," which is the spiritual reality seen from the point of view of God. This spiritual reality is much more than can be grasped through the senses. Because of the limitations of the senses, human beings come to believe in a mind apart from God. However, when the human mind yields to God, the divine Mind, sin and sickness are overcome and human beliefs give way to "man" in the image and likeness of God, whole and perfect. The spiritual reality is immortal and free from evil, whereas human minds are subject to beliefs in sin, sickness, and death. This physical sense of life is a counterfeit of God's spiritual creation. Healing, therefore, is mental and, if needed, involves repentance and regeneration. Medical treatment of illness that does not take into account the mental nature of disease and the need for regenerating the human mind does not reach the real problem that needs healing. Although in reality there is no death, humans "pass on" from one place of existence to another until regeneration effects the needed change.

The Trinity—Father, Son, and Holy Spirit—represents to humanity the divine nature, Life, Truth, and Love. God is immortal Mind (often called Father-Mother God) understood as Spirit, Soul, Life, Truth, Love, and Principle. Jesus was the human embodiment of Christ, the divine idea of sonship with God. He is revered as the Way-shower and master Christian healer. The Holy Spirit is God's own understanding of his relationship to his beloved creation.

Sacred Books/Scriptures

Christian Scientists accept the Bible as their guide to eternal life. Mrs. Eddy said she wrote *Science and Health* under divine inspiration. As its title indicates, it is a key to unlocking the spiritual treasures of the Bible and a resource for spiritual healing. It is considered to be the "pastor" of the church, together with the Bible.

Practices

The Sunday worship service is led by two people (usually a man and a woman)—the First Reader, who conducts the service and reads from *Science and Health*, and the Second Reader, who reads from the Bible. The sermon, which consists of references from the Bible and correlative passages from *Science and Health*, is prepared by the Mother Church and is the same for all branches. Church members read and study this sermon each day of the week prior to the Sunday service and listen to it read as a sermon on Sunday. There is no choir, but hymns reflecting Christian Science theology are sung by the congregation. At Wednesday evening meetings, members give testimonials of Christian Science healing.

There is no ordained clergy. Instead, there are Readers, teachers, and practitioners. Although teachers are relatively few, almost all branches have one or more practitioners. They are professionals who devote their full time to the healing ministry. Practitioners do not give advice or provide personal counseling but treat the patient through prayer endeavoring to bring to light the patient's true spiritual status as the loved child of God. There is an extensive system of instruction in Christian Science, and class instruction is often a requirement for holding many positions in the church. A board of lectureship provides free public lectures throughout the world, sponsored by branch churches. There are also public reading rooms associated with each branch church where anyone may browse the library and read or purchase the Bible, *The Christian Science Monitor*, or other Christian Science publications.

Christian Scientists do not rely on inoculations or vaccinations for preventive cures. (See "Classroom Concerns" below.) They endeavor to reach disease in its incipient stage, which is seen as being mental, and thereby prevent its physical development. However, situations may arise where they submit to inoculations or vaccinations while appealing to Christian Science to avoid any possible negative results. Christian Scientists sometimes accept certain surgical practices, the medical setting of broken bones, dental work, and corrective eyeglasses, although all these conditions have been recorded as being healed through prayer. Christian Scientists report what appear to be infectious or contagious diseases to the health department, but usually rely on Christian Science treatment for healing. Decisions about health care are left to individuals. When relying on Christian Science treatment for healing, God is understood as being the only healer; but if members decide to seek medical treatment, they are not abandoned by their church.

Just as God, the divine Mind, is pure and free from error, so one should maintain good moral practices by avoiding liquor, tobacco, and other harmful substances. With their attention to health and their emphasis on spiritual virtues, Christian Scientists generally have an optimistic view of life and participate fully in social, civic, and economic affairs of their communities.

Main Subgroups

There is only one Church of Christ, Scientist—the Mother Church—located in Boston, Massachusetts, and all local churches throughout the world are branches of the Mother Church.

Common Misunderstandings and Stereotypes

Note: Christian Science should be distinguished from Scientology. Scientology is a twentieth century movement founded by L. Ron Hubbard which is a system of applied religious philosophy. Its purpose is to achieve "a renewed awareness of self as a spiritual and immortal being."[1] Christian Science should also be distinguished from the Church of Religious Science. (See chapter on "New Age Religion.")

"Christian Scientists avoid all medical treatment."
As a rule, this is true, but sometimes Christian Scientists might choose to use medical treatment until their understanding of God's care grows stronger.

"Christian Scientists would rather let their children die than seek medical help."
Cases of this sort have been reported in the press from time to time, and the public often responds with horror and outrage at the insensitivity of parents. But Christian Scientists love their children as much as any parents, and they choose Christian Science treatment not from insensitivity to their children's welfare but because they believe this form of treatment to be the most effective. The death of a child is always tragic and is never seen as the outcome of the way the child was treated. For many, Christian Scientists as well as others, the ability to love their children is grounded in faith. Christian Scientists try to live the very best life they can and to raise their children the best way they know. Legally, the issues concerning the health care choices parents make for their children are complex and have not been resolved completely.

Classroom Concerns

Christian Scientist parents often will present a form at the beginning of the school year requesting accommodations provided by state law with regard to physical examinations, courses of study or parts of courses dealing with certain aspects of health, and immunizations that are contrary to their religious tenets and practices. This form includes directions for treatment other than first aid in the event of illness or injury.

Children may ask to be excused from some classes, especially health courses that include disease symptomatology and medical instruction. This accommodation usually can be provided quietly and privately. Teachers often require these students to do an alternative assignment. Sometimes teachers have asked Christian Science students and parents to share how they deal with health issues, and they are generally happy to do so. This also provides an opportunity to explore how different world views affect people's understanding of health and illness.

Up to the age of 20, children are given instruction in Sunday School in the practice of Christian Science. Although education is valued by Christian Scientists, human knowledge is of relative worth when compared with the truth they claim they find in the Bible and its interpretation in *Science and Health*. If this claim should be expressed in class, it would be an opportunity to explore the multiplicity of truth claims among religious traditions and how people should learn to live together even though they have different religious beliefs.

When a child is injured or appears ill, teachers should consult the school nurse or the parents, who usually have established together a plan for care.

Population Data

No official statistics are released by the Church of Christ, Scientist, but it is known that there are approximately 2,400 branch churches around the world. Kosmin and Lachman[2] found that there are 214,000 adult Christian Scientists in the United States.

—J.H.

Notes

1. L. Ron Hubbard. *The Rediscovery of the Human Soul* (Los Angeles: L. Ron Hubbard Library, 1996), 43.

2. Barry A. Kosmin and Seymour P. Lachman, *One Nation Under God: Religion in Contemporary American Society* (New York: Harmony Books, 1993), 15.

Further Reading

DeWitt, John. *The Christian Science Way of Life*. Boston: Christian Science Publishing, 1971.

Gottschalk, Stephen. *The Emergence of Christian Science in American Religious Life*. Berkeley: University of California Press, 1973.

Peel, Robert. *Christian Science: Its Encounter with American Culture*. New York: Holt, Rinehart & Winston, 1958.

Wilson, Bryan R. *Sects and Society: A Sociological Study of the Elim Tabernacle, Christian Science, and Cristadelphians*. Berkeley and Los Angeles: University of California Press, 1961.

Christianity
Jehovah's Witnesses

Origins

Charles Taze Russell (1852–1916), called Pastor, was the general organizer (Jehovah's Witnesses recognize no human founder) and first president, but it was in 1931 under the second president, Joseph F. Rutherford (1869–1942), called Judge, that the name Jehovah's Witnesses was first used. Russell calculated from evidence in the Bible that the world was in the last days before the Battle of Armageddon. The work of Jehovah's Witnesses is to prepare the world for the consequences of this event. Their headquarters and printing factories are at Bethel in Brooklyn, New York, where they carry on an extensive publishing effort, producing works such as *The Watchtower*, *Awake! Our Kingdom Ministry*, and other pamphlets, books, and brochures. They use these publications for evangelical and doctrinal purposes. The Watchtower Bible and Tract Society of Pennsylvania is incorporated and represents Jehovah's Witnesses legally. The president of this society, together with a group called the Governing Body, determine doctrine and practice.

Beliefs

Jesus Christ, the son of Jehovah God, was a perfect human being who died and was raised as an immortal spirit person. During his earthly life and ministry, he began to select the 144,000 "faithful and discreet slave" class (also called the Bride of Christ). They will rule with him during the thousand-year period called the Millennium. In a certain sense, that period has already begun, for Christ's presence can be recognized even now. Satan has been cast out of heaven and currently rules the world, working his perfidious will through such human institutions as religion, business, and government. Soon, there will occur the Battle of Armageddon, when Satan and his following will be cast into the abyss. The dead, who have been in a state of unconsciousness, will be resurrected and given a second chance. At the end of the Millennium, Satan will return to earth to "deceive the nations" (Rev. 20:8). Then, together with all those who have continued to be willfully wicked, he will be utterly destroyed by fire. The faithful, who resist his assaults, will be granted everlasting life in the flesh on paradise Earth, and Christ will return the rulership of the world to his Father, Jehovah.

Dates have been set for these events (pastor Russell began this process). The most important one is 1914, when the "times of the Gentiles" (which started in the biblical period) ended and the "times of the end" began. Many of the events predicted by Russell and others did not take place, but leaders have been ready and willing to admit their mistakes. They do not claim to be prophets and state that the chronological order is an imperfect tool that is constantly undergoing reevaluation. Nevertheless, they maintain that we are even now in the times of the end.

Sacred Books/Scriptures

The Bible is the sole basis of belief. It is the revealed will of Jehovah God. There is no other creed, dogma, doctrine, or tradition that carries authority, although the many publications, pronouncements, and guidelines of the leaders are consulted regularly as aids to understanding the biblical message.

Practices

Jehovah's Witnesses consider themselves a society, not a denomination or sect, and they meet in Kingdom Halls, not churches. They are organized as a theocracy (a society governed by God), with Jehovah and Christ as the principal rulers, and the president of The Watchtower Bible and Tract Society, together with the Governing Body, as the main governing agents. Local congregations are organized into larger units called circuits, and these in turn are organized into regions. Each congregation is served by a body of elders under the supervision of a circuit overseer. There is no separate clergy, but all members are expected to participate in evangelical ministry. Active members are called publishers. They distribute the Society's literature, witness from door to door, and evangelize those who are not Jehovah's Witnesses. There are also ministerial servants, who work as clerks and attendants, as well as pioneers, who dedicate themselves to full-time evangelical activities.

Baptism is by immersion and is considered a public sign of dedication. Once a year, Jehovah's Witnesses observe The Lord's Supper, or The Lord's Evening Meal, as a memorial. They use no images in their services and pray directly to Jehovah through Christ. Their main activity, as the name implies, is to preach to those who are not Witnesses the "Good News" that God's original earthly paradise will return and those who are saved will receive everlasting life.

Jehovah's Witnesses try to maintain a neutral attitude toward worldly affairs because they believe that the world is controlled by Satan. They keep themselves apart by observing a number of special practices. They do not hold elective office, vote, salute the flag, serve in the military, celebrate holidays or birthdays, or accept blood transfusions. They are submissive to all laws not in conflict with God's law, but they are firm in their conviction that the Bible is the sole authority and model for practice.

Main Subgroups

The main subgroups include Assemblies of the Called Out Ones of Yah, Assemblies of Yah, Assemblies of Yahweh, Assembly of Yahweh, Church of God (Jerusalem), New Life Fellowship, Scripture Research Association, and Yahweh's Assembly in Messiah.

Among other groups that share millennial and separatist views are Seventh-day Adventists, Dawn Bible Students Association, Layman's Home Missionary Movement, and Advent Christian Church.

Common Misunderstandings and Stereotypes

"Jehovah's Witnesses are unpatriotic because they do not salute the flag or perform military service."

Witnesses do not mean to be disrespectful toward any nation, but they believe saluting the flag is an idolatrous act (i.e., the worship of something other than God). Military service, voting, holding public office, and participating in patriotic celebrations are not in keeping with God's law, which admonishes them to stay apart from the world. For this and similar reasons, they also refuse to accept blood transfusions or celebrate birthdays. They have been severely persecuted, punished, and martyred for their attitude toward worldly powers. At the same time, they have had a major influence on constitutional law and on broadening the exercise of civil liberties such as freedom of speech, worship, and the press.

"Door-to-door proselytizing is an annoying invasion of personal privacy and a misguided attempt to force religion on people."

Some people feel that encounters with Jehovah's Witnesses at their front doors are annoying. However, Jehovah's Witnesses are trained in personal evangelizing and believe that their message must reach as many individuals as possible to prepare them for the final struggle. They recognize that people cannot be forced to accept their views, but they are prepared to pay the consequences of affronting some as the price of their dedication and efforts. In fact, they are exercising constitutional freedoms that should be respected as much as any other rights.

"Jehovah's Witnesses are inconsistent, expecting the imminent return of Christ but planning to live in the world at the same time."

Although they have been disappointed a number of times, Jehovah's Witnesses believe and have been assured that there will be a Second Coming of Christ. They rely on their leaders to provide as accurate an account of these anticipated events as possible, recognizing that all such calculations are subject to human error. In the meantime, they avoid contact with worldly institutions that they believe remain under the influence of Satan—other religions, the business world, and government—while following the biblical injunction to provide for themselves and others.

Classroom Concerns

Children of Jehovah's Witnesses are expected to follow biblical practices and avoid saluting the flag, pledging allegiance, standing for the pledge (if by standing they give evidence of participating in the observance), marching in patriotic parades, singing patriotic or school songs, participating in school politics, observing holidays (whether national, religious, or local), celebrating birthdays, participating in extracurricular activities and sports (especially where cheerleading and home-coming activities are involved, or martial arts such as boxing and wrestling are practiced), or taking part in lotteries, games of chance, or gambling. They are also to be carefully selective when asked to join a club or take part in school plays. These and other restrictions are based upon moral and religious principles. There-fore, accommodations should be made for their observance. Jehovah's Witnesses do not mean to be disrespectful, even though other children may ridicule them. It is important that Jehovah's Witnesses not be made to feel left out because of their convictions. If a student is noticed by other students to be following these practices, the teacher could turn this occasion into an important lesson on constitutional rights and freedoms.

Jehovah's Witnesses do not give or accept blood transfusions. They follow the Bible, which commands that they abstain from blood because it is the life God gives to humans (Lev. 17:10–14). School nurses should know the particular preferences of Jehovah's Witnesses families regarding the kind of medical treatment to be administered to their children.

The views of Jehovah's Witnesses regarding Christian history, the nature of God and Jesus Christ, and what will happen in the future may not be the same as other Christian or non-Christian views. For Jehovah's Witnesses, their history is a sacred, true, and meaningful account of the world that includes an understanding of the nature of human life and its ultimate destiny as the Bible has foretold. If this difference should come up in class, teachers might use the occasion to teach cultural diversity and toleration of different viewpoints.

Population Data

Kosmin and Lachman[1] report an adult population of 1,381,000 Jehovah's Witnesses in the United States.

—J.H.

Notes

1. Barry A. Kosmin and Seymour P. Lachman, *One Nation Under God: Religion in Contemporary American Society* (New York: Harmony Books, 1993), 15.

Further Reading

Beckford, James A. *The Trumpet of Prophecy: A Sociological Study of Jehovah's Witnesses.* Oxford: Basil Blackwell, 1975.

Harrison, Barbara G. *Visions of Glory: A History and a Memory of Jehovah's Witnesses.* New York: Simon & Schuster, 1978.

Penton, James. *Apocalypse Delayed: The Story of Jehovah's Witnesses.* Toronto: University of Toronto Press, 1985.

Christianity

Mormonism/Church of Jesus Christ of Latter-day Saints

Origins

Joseph Smith Jr. founded the Church of Jesus Christ of Latter-day Saints in 1830 in Fayette, New York. Smith said that he was visited by God the Father and his son Jesus Christ, who commanded him to "restore" the ancient church, which, Mormons believe, was originally established by Jesus Christ. Smith and his followers faced persecution because of their beliefs and moved from their original homes, first to Ohio, then Missouri, and finally to Illinois. There, he and a brother were murdered while under protective custody. Under a new leader, Brigham Young, a major branch of Mormons moved west to Salt Lake Valley, Utah, and in 1847 established the headquarters of the Church of Jesus Christ of Latter-day Saints. Although accustomed to the appellation Mormon, most followers refer to themselves as Latter-day Saints, or sometimes simply Saints.

Beliefs

Mormons accept the basic beliefs of Christianity. Their understanding of the "restored gospel" is that the Godhead consists of three separate, distinct beings: God the Father, his son Jesus Christ (who are beings of flesh and bone), and the Holy Ghost. There is no original sin, but humans are held individually responsible for their actions, and transgressions will be punished. All except a few "sons of perdition" will be saved to one of three kingdoms, but only those who are faithful in all things will be exalted to the highest kingdom, the Celestial Kingdom. To reach the Celestial Kingdom, a person must perform works—which include holding church positions and diligently rendering good to others—gain knowledge, repent, receive baptism by immersion for remission of sins, and receive the laying on of hands

48

for the gift of the Holy Ghost. Those who die faithful will continue to progress spiritually until they become like God, who is our literal Father in Heaven (we have a Mother in Heaven also). Because human beings were born of Heavenly Parents as spirit children before they were born on earth to mortal parents, it is the destiny of the faithful to become like their Heavenly Parents. To become a Heavenly Parent eternally requires that men and women be bound in marriage. Faithfulness means, among other things, being sealed in marriage for all eternity, an act that can be performed only in Mormon temples. This practice demonstrates the enormous importance the Mormon faith places on the family. Those who are not married may qualify themselves for the Celestial Kingdom, but—unlike those who are married—cannot become like God.

For Mormons, history begins with the creation of the world, and the events of the past 200 years are part of that ongoing history. God continues to reveal himself; formerly to the prophet Joseph Smith, and now to the subsequent Mormon Church presidents.

According to Smith's *Articles of Faith*, Mormon belief also includes: the gift of tongues, visions, and healing; being subject to the laws and government of the country; the free exercise of conscience and the right of all people to worship as they choose; being honest, true, chaste, benevolent, and virtuous; and doing good to everyone.

Sacred Books/Scriptures

The Book of Mormon is equal in status to the Bible as the revealed word of God, according to Mormons, and is the record of a sacred history that began in 600 B.C.E. when a prophet in Jerusalem named Lehi led his followers to North America under God's direction. Soon after their arrival in North America, the followers of Lehi began to keep records on metal plates. Subsequently, conflict ensued, which divided Lehi's expanding offspring into two groups, one of which became the ancestors of the Native Americans. From the time of Lehi to Christ's crucifixion, the Savior's birth and atonement were explicitly prophesied in the Book of Mormon. Christ, after his resurrection, visited North America (the New World) and established his church there. The Book of Mormon ends at about the year 420 C.E. with Moroni [muh-ROHN-eye], a descendant of those who survived the final destruction of his people. Moroni received from his father, Mormon, an abridgment of the plates begun under Lehi and eventually buried them at a place in New York (state) called Hill Cumorah. Then, in the "latter days," Moroni returned as an angel and revealed their location to Joseph Smith, who translated them as the Book of Mormon. For Mormons, the Book of Mormon is a "second witness" of the divinity of Jesus Christ.

Practices

Deseret (meaning "honey bee"), Utah's original name in The Book of Mormon, aptly describes the Mormon Church, which is a beehive of activity. It is run by the president, who is called Prophet, and several bodies of officers that counsel, supervise, and preside over its various parts. There is no official clergy, but every male is eligible to hold either the Melchizedek (higher) priesthood or the Aaronic (lesser) priesthood. All officers serve without pay, except those few in full-time leadership positions. At age 12, boys are ordained to a priesthood office and are expected to assume duties of service to the church.

Activities include:

1. **Family Life**. The family is the most important unit of the church. A notable activity of family life is the moral and spiritual education of the children. They are taught to refrain from tobacco, alcohol, tea, and coffee; observe a healthy diet; abide by church dress codes; engage in regular exercise; and act with moderation. Careful attention is paid to sexual morality because of the example set by the Heavenly Parents: in giving birth to preexistent human beings, they established marriage as the perfect and only context for sexual activity. Monday is Family Home Evening, a time for education, discussion, and recreation.

   Families donate one-tenth of their annual income to the church. In addition, they make a fast offering each month and donate to the needy the cost of the two meals not eaten. Families are urged to provision themselves with at least one year's supply of the basic needs of food, clothing, and shelter.

   Women serve central roles as wives and mothers, although they are active in other areas of the church as well. After baptism, at age 8 or so, sons accompany their fathers to meetings and begin taking an active role in the church.

2. **Mission**. At about age 19, young men are called to serve missions; young women may serve missions as well. In pairs, the missionaries are sent to various parts of the world, including locations in the United States, for a period of two years, where they bring the Mormon message to those who are willing to listen (those who are "honest in heart").

3. **Ward Activity**. The church is divided into areas, regions, stakes (geographical divisions), and wards (local churches or parishes). Ward activities include weekly worship, social events, classes, and welfare projects. The church sponsors and encourages participation in many cultural events (the Mormon Tabernacle Choir is justly famous). The church is committed to doing good throughout the world and is active in charities and international welfare projects. It is organized to meet all the needs of its members, having its own newspaper, television station, real estate services, banks, insurance companies, and department stores.

4. **Temple Work**. Temples are not places for Sunday worship; they are places for marriage, baptism, and other forms of church work, such as baptism for the dead. After a temple is dedicated, it is closed to all but Mormons in good standing who have been approved by their bishops.

5. **Genealogy**. Those who have died without hearing the restored Gospel may receive vicarious baptism, which is carried out by members who stand proxy for them. Because the dead must be identified individually, an extensive genealogical library in Salt Lake City has come into existence where searches can be made. However, baptism does not guarantee salvation because even the dead are free to choose whether or not to accept it.

Main Subgroups

Although the Church of Jesus Christ of Latter-day Saints is the largest body of Mormons, there are several groups that differ from it doctrinally or practically. These are the Church of Christ (Temple Lot); Church of Jesus Christ (Bickertonites); Church of Jesus Christ of Latter-day Saints (Strangite); and Reorganized Church of Jesus Christ of Latter-day Saints.

Common Misunderstandings and Stereotypes

"Mormons practice polygamy."

In 1852, the church admitted the practice of polygamy, calling it celestial or plural marriage. The purpose was a religious one: to raise a righteous generation to greet Jesus Christ at the Second Coming. Polygamy was not against federal law until 1862 and, even after that, it was defended as a religious right under First Amendment protection. After much persecution, the church officially discontinued plural marriage in 1890. This decision was coincident with a new turn in church history, whereby millennial and separatist views were forfeited in favor of participation in the larger community.

"Mormons do not allow African Americans to be members of the priesthood."

Although this was true in the past, in 1978 it was revealed and ruled that the "long-promised day" had come: every faithful, worthy man in the church could receive the holy priesthood, with power to exercise its divine authority.

"Mormons are not Christian."

Mormons believe that salvation depends upon knowing Christ. They understand themselves to be Christians and their church to be the only legitimate church of Jesus Christ. However, the Mormon understanding of salvation and cosmic history is sufficiently distinct that some consider them another branch of Christianity in addition to Protestant, Catholic, and Orthodox Christians.

"The story of Joseph Smith translating gold plates found on Hill Cumorah cannot be proved."

As an instance of sacred stories, the existence of the plates can be no more (or less) proved than many other religious "facts." For Mormons, their history is a sacred, true, and meaningful account of the whole of creation, including the nature and destiny of human and divine life and the historical and eternal relationships among all human beings, living and dead. These considerations supersede questions of proof.

"Door-to-door proselytizing is an annoying invasion of personal privacy and resented for its attempt to force religion on people."

Mormons on mission understand their efforts to be educational, and the householder always has a free choice to accept the message or not. That people may resent being evangelized is something Mormons accept as the price they must pay for their efforts.

Classroom Concerns

Mormons look after the moral and spiritual education of their children with great care. Mormon students sometimes may appear unresponsive in the classroom with sex education and other morally sensitive topics. This is not out of disrespect or lack of interest, but because children already have been taught at home. The teacher could use this as an opportunity to explore the plurality of ethical codes.

Some Mormon students may want to be excused from evening activities such as homework or school events, particularly on Monday, which is Family Home Evening. Because active participation in church life is expected, students need to organize their weekly schedule so that homework, for example, can be done during those times when they are not busy with church activities.

Mormon understanding of history may not be the same as other Christian or non-Christian views. If this difference should come up in class, teachers may use the occasion to teach cultural diversity and toleration of different viewpoints.

Population Data

As of 1995, there were 9.3 million Mormons worldwide. More than half of all Mormons live outside North America. Kosmin and Lachman[1] list the adult Mormons in the United States at 2,487,000. Including children, this would translate into a total United States Mormon population of 4 to 5 million.

—J.H.

Notes

1. Barry A. Kosmin and Seymour P. Lachman, *One Nation Under God: Religion in Contemporary American Society* (New York: Harmony Books, 1993), 15.

Further Reading

Arrington, Leonard, and Davis Bitton. *The Mormon Experience: A History of the Latter-day Saints.* New York: Alfred A. Knopf, 1979.

Bushman, Richard L. *Joseph Smith and the Beginnings of Mormonism.* Urbana: University of Illinois Press, 1984.

Moore, Laurence. *Religious Outsiders and the Making of Americans.* New York: Oxford University Press, 1986.

Shipps, Jan. *Mormonism: The Story of a New Religious Tradition.* Urbana and Chicago: University of Illinois Press, 1985.

Christianity

Orthodox Christianity (Eastern Orthodoxy)

Origins

The Orthodox ("right doctrine/worship") Church traces its origins to the churches founded by the apostles in the Middle East and the Balkans in the first century. Additionally, the church's roots are in the Christianity of the Byzantine or Eastern Roman Empire. As the church developed in the early centuries, seven ecumenical or all-embracing councils were held at which the bishops of the entire church assembled to discuss and clarify matters of belief and practice. These seven councils were held at cities in what is now Turkey: Nicaea (325 C.E.). Constantinople I (now Istanbul) (381), Ephesus (431), Chalcedon (451), Constantinople II (553), Constantinople III (680), and Nicaea II (787). The councils determined the basic creed of Christianity on such points as the nature of Jesus as both God and man; the nature of the Trinity of Father, Son, and Holy Spirit (three persons in one God); and the role of Mary as Mother of God. Though other councils were held later, they involved only the Roman Catholic church and are therefore not considered legitimate by the Orthodox.

Beliefs

Like other Christians, the Orthodox affirm the role of Jesus as Messiah (Hebrew *Mashiach* ["anointed one"] whose Greek equivalent is *Christos* [Christ]) who sanctified or redeemed the human race from its estrangement from God. Orthodox Christians believe that Jesus is the Son of God whose life, death, and resurrection confirm his status as both fully human and fully divine. They affirm the doctrine of the Trinity whereby the one God is experienced in three Persons—Father, Son, and Holy Spirit. They believe as well in the doctrine of Christ's triumphant return to judge living and dead at the end of time, in an afterlife with God for the righteous, and of permanent estrangement from God for the wicked.

The Orthodox church considers itself the one true, visible church (a belief also held by Roman Catholicism). It sees itself as a fellowship of churches that developed in the Byzantine Empire, originally under four patriarchates (governing church fatherships): Constantinople, Alexandria, Antioch, and Jerusalem. There was a fifth, Rome, but it separated from the Eastern patriarchates in 1054. (The reasons for the split or schism are complex but centered mainly in the claim of the pope or bishop of Rome to be the head of the entire church rather than simply one of the five patriarchs.) Despite the separation, Orthodox and Catholic Christians recognize the validity of each other's sacraments and call each other "sister churches."

There is no one individual leader in Orthodoxy comparable to the pope in Roman Catholicism. Instead, there are various patriarchates and self-governing churches (of which there are now 15; see "Main Subgroups" below). The patriarch of Constantinople does have "primacy of honor" within the church, but this is not a supreme authority. The structure of the Orthodox church, like that of the Roman Catholic church, is hierarchical: the bishop leads his community—the body of Christ—in teaching true doctrine, administering the sacraments, and making eternal salvation possible.

In other respects, the Orthodox church resembles Roman Catholicism and Protestantism in its basic beliefs—these three principal branches of Christianity all accept the decrees of the first seven church councils (see "Origins" above).

Sacred Books/Scriptures

Orthodoxy, like Roman Catholicism and Protestantism, accepts the Old and New Testaments but uses the Septuagint or Greek version of the Old Testament as its official text. It contains a number of books not found in the Hebrew version used by Jews and Protestants. These additional books in the canon of the Old Testament are: Tobit; Judith; the Additions to the Book of Esther; the Wisdom of Solomon; Ecclesiasticus or the Wisdom of Jesus Son of Sirach; Baruch; the Letter of Jeremiah; the Prayer of Azariah and the Song of the Three Jews; Susanna; Bel and the Dragon; 1–2 Maccabees (all of which Catholics also accept as scriptural); and these other books (not accepted by Catholics): 1 Esdras, the Prayer of Manasseh, Psalm 151, and 3 Maccabees.

Practices

Orthodox Christians practice seven sacraments (the same as Catholics): baptism, chrismation (confirmation), Eucharist (Mass/Holy Communion), confession, holy orders (the ordination ritual of deacons, priests, and bishops), marriage, and the anointing of the sick. Orthodox Christians baptize by a triple immersion of the child in water (unlike Catholics, who baptize by sprinkling water on the child's forehead). Chrismation occurs immediately after baptism (for Catholics, confirmation usually occurs at about age 12). The Eucharist is central to Orthodoxy and is performed in four different rites or styles, with that of St. John Chrysostom the most popular. The other three Eucharistic styles—which do not differ significantly from that of St. John Chrysostom—are those of St. Basil (used during the Sundays of Lent), of

Gregory the Great, and of the Pre-Santified. Eucharist ceremony includes abundant use of incense, candles, chanting, and the wearing of ornate vestments by the priest. Orthodoxy (unlike Roman Catholicism) permits divorce as a last resort.

Priests may marry (unlike Roman Catholicism) but must do so before their ordination; otherwise, they must remain celibate. Bishops may not marry and are usually chosen from the ranks of the monastic communities (who are celibate by virtue of their vow of chastity). Since the fourth century, monasticism (the disciplined life of monks or nuns) has been very important to the church. Unlike western monasticism, there are no religious orders but rather individual communities with their own rules.

Orthodox Christians venerate icons (flat paintings) as a way of honoring Christ, Mary, and the saints. Orthodox churches, as well as Bibles and religious writings, contain such icons.

Orthodox Christians celebrate Christmas on January 7 because they follow a calendar different from that of Catholics and Protestants. The date of Easter sometimes coincides with the date observed by Catholics and Protestants but not always, because the Orthodox stipulate that Easter must always come before the start of the Jewish festival of Passover. The Orthodox New Year is September 1 and marks the start of the cycle of holy days for the church year. Additionally, many of the Orthodox customarily celebrate the New Year on January 1.

Main Subgroups

Orthodoxy consists of 15 self-governing churches: Constantinople, Antioch, Alexandria, Jerusalem, Russia, Serbia, Georgia, Romania, Bulgaria (all headed by patriarchs); and Greece, Cyprus, Albania, Poland, the former Czechoslovakia, and the United States (headed by archbishops/metropolitans). There are also so-called autonomous churches in Japan, Finland, and Crete that lack full independence. In the United States, Orthodox Christians from many of these national churches have formed an umbrella organization, the Standing Conference of Orthodox Bishops of America.

Two Eastern Christian churches, which some might even consider to be fourth and fifth branches of Christianity, are closely allied with the Orthodox Christianity: the Assyrian Church, which stresses the humanity of Christ (to the detriment of his divinity, in the view of the other Christian churches); and the Oriental Orthodox Church, which stresses Jesus' divinity (to the detriment of his humanity, say the other Christian churches). The Oriental Orthodox Church includes Coptic/Egyptian, Ethiopic, Armenian, and Syrian subdivisions.

Common Misunderstandings and Stereotypes

"All Orthodox Christians in the United States are Greek or Russian in origin."
Orthodox Christians come from many countries (see "Main Subgroups" above). Moreover, many persons of other ethnic and religious backgrounds have converted to Orthodoxy, and so Orthodoxy today is an American religion, though with historical ties to various European or Asian mother churches.

"Orthodox Christians are foreigners with little interest in this country. "
Americans of many ethnic and national backgrounds—including Greeks, Russians, and others who are Orthodox—have a natural interest in the countries from which they or their ancestors came. Still, they chose to come to the United States and are as loyal as any other Americans. (This stereotype is applicable to many of the religions discussed in this book.)

"Orthodox Christians worship icons. "
As explained in "Practices" (above), icons are only symbolic representations meant to inspire devotion to Christ, Mary, and the saints. The icons themselves are not worshipped.

Classroom Concerns

It is suggested that teachers familiarize themselves with the dates of the Orthodox holy days (see Appendix B for a calendar).
Because Roman Catholicism and Orthodoxy are similar in so many respects, it is important to clarify the distinctions when teaching about Christianity.

Population Data

There are about 370 million Orthodox Christians worldwide, of whom about 4.5 million reside in the United States. Additionally, there are 17 million Assyrian and Oriental Orthodox worldwide, of whom 500,000 reside in the United States.[1]

—B.H.

Notes

1.   Robert Famighetti, ed. *World Almanac and Book of Facts* (New York: World Almanac Books/Funk & Wagnalls, 1997), 646.

Further Reading

Harakas, Stanley S. *The Orthodox Church: 455 Questions and Answers*. Brookline, MA: Holy Cross Orthodox Press, 1988.

Meyendorff, John. *The Orthodox Church*. Crestwood, NY: St. Vladimir's Seminary Press, 1981.

Ware, Timothy. *The Orthodox Church*. New York: Penguin Books, 1983.

Christianity

Protestantism

Origins

There is no "Church of Protestantism" but instead a group of churches that trace their origins to the Protestant Reformation. Thus, Protestant Christianity began in the sixteenth century as a reform movement within the Roman Catholic Church. Although there had been reforms before, Martin Luther (1483–1546), a German priest, was the first Protestant reformer. He wanted to change the Roman Catholic Church's beliefs and practices. For him, humans were sinful and incapable of achieving their own salvation. He accused the church of corruption because it promised salvation through the sale of indulgences. Luther's reformation led to the separation of Protestant churches from the Roman Catholic Church.

Under King Henry VIII, the Church of England (Anglican Church) also separated from the Roman Catholic Church. Puritans, in their turn, wanted to cleanse the Anglican Church of all vestiges of Catholicism. Even further, separatist or independent Puritans concluded that reformation from within was impossible, and they created their own churches. They fled England for Holland, and then to North America, where, as Pilgrims at Plymouth Colony, they signed the Mayflower Compact, uniting church and state "for the glory of God." Non-separating Puritans also came to North America looking for a purified Church of England, but in the long run created their own (Congregational) churches. The separatist spirit appeared also in Rhode Island, where Baptists reacted strongly against church-state union. Anglicans, Quakers, Mennonites, Presbyterians, and Dutch Reformed settled in other colonies. The Great Awakening, a revival movement beginning in the eighteenth century, preached a message of personal salvation. Methodism, at first an evangelical effort within the Anglican Church in the eighteenth century, became a separate church and contributed to the revivalist spirit.

Protestant movements in the United States continued to proliferate in the nineteenth century, stimulated by the disestablishment of churches and the consequent freedom of religious choice. Major denominations were joined by non-denominational Christian churches. Other movements deriving from Protestantism during this period include: Transcendentalism and Unitarian Universalism; occult and spiritualist groups; Mormonism and Christian Science; African American churches; Millenialists (who expected the imminent return of Christ); and utopian communities (Shakers, Oneida Community). In the twentieth century, Social Gospel, Pentecostal, fundamentalist Christian, New Age, and Charismatic movements have added to the complexity of the religious scene in the United States.

Beliefs

Like other Christians, Protestants affirm the role of Jesus as Messiah (Hebrew *Mashiach* ["anointed one"] whose Greek equivalent is *Christos* [Christ]) who redeemed the human race from its estrangement from God. Protestants believe that Jesus is the Son of God whose life, death, and resurrection confirm his status as both fully human and fully divine. They affirm the doctrine of the Trinity whereby the one God is experienced in three Persons—Father, Son, and Holy Spirit. They believe as well in the doctrine of Christ's triumphant return to judge living and dead at the end of time and in an afterlife with God for the righteous and of permanent estrangement from God for the wicked.

Most Protestants also subscribe to the following beliefs which distinguish them from Catholic and Orthodox Christians:

1. Salvation is by the grace of God through faith alone, rather than by human effort.

2. The Bible is the sole authority for faith, rather than church traditions or rituals.

3. God is sovereign and decides who will be saved.

4. Humans are sinful and cannot achieve salvation by their own efforts.

5. All believers have direct access to God without the mediation of the church.

6. All life and work is a sacred Christian vocation, in addition to the work of the church.

7. Nothing in the world, only God, is worthy of worship.

Sacred Books/Scriptures

The Christian Bible contains the Old Testament (equivalent to the Hebrew Bible) and the New Testament, a collection of narratives, letters, and writings about the life of Jesus and his Apostles. Some Protestant denominations recognize the Apocrypha or "hidden" books as being scriptural. The Apocrypha includes 1–2

Esdras, Tobit, Judith, the Additions to Esther, Wisdom of Solomon, Ecclesiasticus (Sirach), Baruch, Letter of Jeremiah, Prayer of Azariah and Song of the Three Young Men, Susanna, Bel and the Dragon, the Prayer of Manasseh, and 1–2 Maccabees. Certain groups—such as Mormons and Christian Scientists—supplement the Bible with their own writings. There are at least three Protestant views regarding the Bible: (1) it was created by humans but under God's direct inspiration; (2) it contains the literal words of God, recorded without error by human hands; or (3) it is the work of fallible humans struggling to write a divine story in limited human language. Also, there are numerous English translations. Each denomination uses a version that reflects their particular understanding of God and history.

Practices

Most Protestants practice weekly or semiweekly congregational worship, observe the major Christian holy days, and permit clergy to marry. Worship may be elaborate and liturgical (e.g., Lutherans) or simple and without ritual (e.g., Quakers). Most Protestants recognize only two sacraments, baptism and the Lord's Supper (Eucharist). Some Protestants believe that the sacraments are sources of divine grace, while others believe them to be memorials of the redemptive work of Christ.

The weekly worship service usually includes: congregational and choral singing, prayer, Bible readings, preaching, confession of faith, sacraments (baptism, Lord's Supper/Eucharist), and collection of tithes and offerings.

As the word *protestant* suggests, in principle there is a critical tension between Protestants and the social status quo. For some, the world is corrupt and will be saved only by the return of Christ to earth. They take little part in social and political matters. Others believe the world is in a constant state of renewal at the hand of God. Their task is to help bring about this renewal by working actively in society.

Main Subgroups

Subgroups, with typical examples, include:

Adventist (Seventh-day Adventists; Jehovah's Witnesses). Strong conviction that the end of the world will occur in the very near future and that they must be prepared for this event. (See the chapters "Seventh-day Adventists" and "Jehovah's Witnesses" for more detail.).

Baptist (Christian Church [Disciples of Christ]; Baptist). Practice adult baptism. Stress complete separation of church and state, with emphasis on religious freedom and personal conscience (not to be confused with Anabaptists of the Radical Reformed tradition; see below).

Christian Science (Church of Christ, Scientist). Believe God is Spirit, and human beings are immortal and free from evil. It is only when human beings believe in a mind apart from God that they become subject to sin, sickness, and death. Treatment by prayer is preferred to medical treatment. (See the chapter "Christian Science" for more detail.)

Communal (Amana Community; Amish; Shakers). Communities exist entirely apart from the larger society and often include a strong leader, a strong system of social control, and economic self-sufficiency.

Episcopal (called the Episcopal Church in the United States; the Anglican Church in Canada, England, and elsewhere). Similar to Roman Catholic—stressing Bible, tradition, and reason—except ruled by bishops rather than the pope. The Book of Common Prayer contains the major doctrines and guidelines for worship.

Evangelical-Fundamentalist (Plymouth Brethren; Independent Bible Churches). Believe in a personal experience of salvation through Jesus Christ; biblical inerrancy; different historical ages or dispensations during which God renews his efforts to save the world; imminent return of Christ (Second Advent); strict ethical practices in contrast to laxness of modernity; restoration of purity of early church independent of denominations; and the church as a fellowship of the saved. (See also the chapter "Fundamentalism.")

Holiness (Church of the Nazarene; Churches of God). Reject worldliness and advocate a strict code of behavior. Believe in "second blessing": after being born again, one grows in grace until perfected in holiness or sanctification.

Liberal (American Ethical Union; Unitarian Universalists). Believe that human ability and intelligence is able to bring about a better world; the Bible is understood through modern methods of history, literary criticism, and archaeology; acceptance of scientific, evolutionary view of origins of the world; toleration of many views of salvation and various Christian doctrines.

Lutheran (American Lutheran Church; Lutheran Church—Missouri Synod). Because of human sinfulness, salvation is not merited and cannot be earned; salvation is by the grace of God through faith alone, rather than faith and works, as the Catholic Church teaches; bread and wine of the Eucharist are not replaced by the body and blood of Christ (transubstantiation), as in Catholic practice, nor is the Lord's Supper considered a symbolic remembrance, as in other Protestant practices, but Christ is present everywhere, His body and blood being especially present along with the bread and wine in the Eucharist (consubstantiation).

Methodist (United Methodists; African Methodist Episcopal). Orderly organization and living are combined with emphasis on direct religious experience; all people can receive the grace of God and are eligible for sanctification or freedom from sin.

Mormon (Church of Jesus Christ of Latter-day Saints). Mormons believe that their founder, Joseph Smith, discovered sacred tablets in 1830 that comprise the Book of Mormon. Equal in status to the Bible, it is the record of a sacred history dating to 600 B.C.E. when Lehi, a prophet in Jerusalem, led his followers to North America under God's direction. Mormon theology differs in several respects from that of other Protestants. (See the chapter "Mormonism" for more detail.)

Pentecostal-Charismatic (Assemblies of God; Church of God). Believe in personal ecstatic experience of the Holy Spirit; manifestations of Holy Spirit through speaking in tongues and healing; biblical inerrancy; baptism of the Holy Spirit subsequent to conversion; imminent return of Christ.

Radical Reformed (Mennonites; Quakers). Mennonites and other Anabaptists practice adult baptism; oppose taking oaths, military service, or holding public office; believe in strict separation from the state, strict adherence to the Bible, and the fellowship of believers. Quakers are free of church organization, creed, doctrine, and sacrament; God is a real presence within each person; and worship typically is silent fellowship punctuated by individual witness or prayer.

Reformed-Presbyterian (Presbyterian; United Church of Christ). Presbyterians are governed by elected elders or presbyters; believe humans are sinful and saved only by God, who chooses those he wants for eternal life; faith and a good life are the fruits of salvation. The United Church of Christ (Congregational) is governed by the consent of the people, and in theology is similar to Presbyterian. Two other offshoots of Presbyterianism are the liberal Christian Church (Disciples of Christ) and the conservative Church of Christ.

Protestantism in Canada. Protestantism in Canada parallels its United States counterpart denominations with one important exception: In 1925, the Methodist Church in Canada, the Congregationalist Union of Canada, 70 percent of Canada's Presbyterians, and the General Council of Union Churches joined together to form the United Church of Canada (UCC). In 1968, they were joined by the Evangelical United Brethren.

Common Misunderstandings and Stereotypes

"All religions are similar to Protestant Christianity."

In this uncritical view, to be religious means to practice weekly worship of God in a church, in hope of salvation from sin and with the promise of eternal life. It includes the exercise of moral conscience, free choice regarding which church to attend, the freedom to believe in religion even though others may not (or not to believe even though others may), and, often, a deeply emotional experience of salvation. Although this is certainly true of Protestant Christianity, one can find among the religions of the world those that have no weekly worship, no God, no church, no idea of salvation from sin, no notion of eternal life, no religiously based moral conscience, no freedom of choice, and no emotion—yet they are religions and should be respected as such.

"Christians are different from Catholics."

Some Protestants avoid labels altogether, wishing only to be called Christian. Because Protestants are different from Catholics, it may seem that Christians also are different. Yet Catholics are Christian. The distinction should be between *Catholic* and *Protestant* Christians.

"Protestants know what they believe. People who don't know their beliefs aren't religious."

Because many Protestant churches are confessional, having written statements of belief and practice, knowledge of these verbal codes may appear as the essence of the religion. Therefore, when followers of other religions are asked what they believe and sometimes are unable to answer, an erroneous conclusion is that they do not know their own religion. However, religions are composed of stories, myths, rituals, and symbols, as well as beliefs, and it is impossible to reduce all of these to linguistic formulae.

Classroom Concerns

With more than 300 branches, Protestant Christianity may appear confusing. Common to all, though, is a concern about ultimate values and a critical attitude toward popular morality. Exploring how Protestant Christianity has dealt with society is one way of teaching critical thinking.

Different Protestant groups approach the Bible differently. Some believe in divine inspiration, while others treat it as they would any other book. But controversy over the Bible should not be an excuse for avoiding it. Of course, as a topic of study in the classroom, the Bible must be used for educational, not religious, purposes. It should be treated fairly, as one would treat any sacred book, whether the Qur'an of Islam or the Bhagavad Gita of Hinduism.

Some Protestants may not want their children to salute the flag and others may practice vegetarianism. For particular restrictions, see the chapters "Jehovah's Witnesses," "Seventh-day Adventists," "Christian Science," and "Mormonism."

Some Protestants advocate prayer in schools. This is a difficult issue, because it pits the principle of separation of church and state against that of freedom of worship. Current practice allows prayer when it is not disruptive or does not compel others to participate.

Some Protestants advocate teaching creationism—treating the biblical creation story as scientific theory—along with evolution. This is also a difficult issue because of ambiguities in defining words such as *fact*, *science*, and *theory*. Current practice allows teaching creationism in comparative religion or history/social studies classes, but not in science.

Population Data

There are more than 300 Protestant churches and denominations in the United States, with more than 72 million members. The largest are:

Baptist, 21 million

Methodist, 8.7 million

Lutheran, 5 million

Mormon, 4 million

Churches of Christ, 3 million

Episcopal, 2.4 million

Presbyterian, 2.8 million

Kosmin and Lachman[1] estimate the combined adult population of Protestants (i.e., the total of all adult Protestants from all denominations) to be about 105 million.

—J.H.

Notes

1.   Barry A. Kosmin and Seymour P. Lachman, *One Nation Under God: Religion in Contemporary American Society* (New York: Harmony Books, 1993), 15–16.

Further Reading

Brown, Robert McAfee. *The Spirit of Protestantism.* New York: Oxford University Press, 1961.

Gaustad, Edwin. *Religious History of America.* New York: Harper & Row, 1974.

Mead, Frank S. *Handbook of Denominations in the United States, New Tenth Edition.* Revised by Samuel S. Hill. Nashville, TN: Abingdon Press, 1995.

Rosten, Leo, ed. *Religions of America.* New York: Simon & Schuster, 1975.

Christianity

Roman Catholicism

Origins

Roman Catholics (from the Greek *catholicos*, "universal") trace their origins to Jesus' disciple Peter, first bishop of Rome, and to his successor bishops who became known as the Holy Father (Italian: "Papa"; English: "Pope") or "Vicar of Christ on Earth." Although there were other important bishops in the early church in such Eastern Mediterranean cities as Athens, Antioch, Alexandria, and Constantinople (now Istanbul), the Roman bishop was the clear leader among the Western bishops. Gradually his authority grew in both the ecclesiastical (church) and secular spheres and he became recognized in the West—and to a lesser extent in the East—as the "first among equals." The Eastern (Orthodox) Church ceased to recognize his authority in any sense after 1054 C.E., when the pope and the patriarch of Constantinople mutually excommunicated each other and the Orthodox Church and Roman Catholic Church separated. (These excommunications were lifted by mutual agreement in 1964.)

Beliefs

The essential beliefs of Roman Catholic Christians are similar to those of the two other major divisions of Christianity, Orthodox and Protestant; there is more agreement than disagreement. Like other Christians, Catholics affirm the role of Jesus as Messiah (Hebrew *Mashiach* ["anointed one"] whose Greek equivalent is *Christos* [Christ]) who redeemed the human race from its estrangement from God. Catholics believe that Jesus is the Son of God whose life, death, and resurrection confirm his status as both fully human and fully divine. They affirm the doctrine of the Trinity whereby the one God is experienced in three Persons—Father, Son, and Holy Spirit. They believe as well in the doctrine of Christ's triumphant return to judge living and dead at the end of time and in an afterlife with God for the righteous and of permanent estrangement from God for the wicked. Differences appear mainly on matters of Church governance and specific practices, such as:

1. Only Catholics recognize the pope's leadership of the college of bishops and his role as Christ's representative on earth. They also believe that when he speaks officially on a matter of faith or moral teaching, he cannot err (the doctrine of papal infallibility).

2. Only Catholics continue to convene the bishops of the entire church for ecumenical councils to discuss matters of belief and practice. There have been 21 such councils in the Catholic Church's history, the most recent being the Second Vatican Council (1962–65). Eastern Orthodox Christians and many Protestant denominations recognize the first seven of these councils.

3. Catholics, like Orthodox Christians, accept the authority both of the Bible and of tradition (i.e., the traditional teaching of the church by the pope and/or the bishops, or as found in the documents of the ecumenical councils).

4. Only Catholics require that priests/ministers remain celibate (Orthodox Christianity requires celibacy solely of its bishops).

5. Only Catholics forbid divorce under any circumstances (though the practice of granting annulments—a declaration that no marriage existed in the first place, enabling a civilly divorced couple to remarry—has become widespread in the past quarter century).

6. Like the Orthodox but unlike Protestants, Catholics revere the Virgin Mary, mother of Jesus, with great fervor. In the doctrine of the Immaculate Conception, they believe that she was conceived without "original sin" (a sort of alienation from God caused by Adam and Eve's original disobedience). There are holy days in her honor (see "Practices" below) and shrines at locations in several countries commemorating appearances by her to devotees (e.g., Lourdes, France; Fatima, Portugal; Guadeloupe, Mexico).

7. Catholic and Orthodox Christians recognize seven sacraments (baptism, the Eucharist, confirmation, reconciliation/penance, matrimony, holy orders, anointing of the sick); most Protestants accept only baptism and the Eucharist. Catholics take a strict view of Christ's presence in the Eucharistic bread and wine. Referred to as the "real presence" or transubstantiation, this doctrine holds that the entire substance of the bread and wine is changed into the body and blood of Christ. Orthodox Christians simply say that Christ is present in the Eucharist with no further philosophical distinctions. Protestants have held several positions on the Eucharist from consubstantiation (Christ is present in, with, and under the presence of bread and wine) to a symbolic presence where the bread and wine remain but symbolize Christ's presence. Baptism is performed by sprinkling water on the candidate's forehead. Confirmation is usually administered at the beginning of adolescence.

Sacred Books/Scriptures

The Bible used by Catholics is virtually identical to that used by other Christians. The exceptions are 12 deuterocanonical (added later to the canon or official list) books accepted as canonical by Catholics: Tobit; Judith; the Additions to the Book of Esther; the Wisdom of Solomon; Ecclesiasticus or the Wisdom of Jesus Son of Sirach; Baruch; the Letter of Jeremiah; the Prayer of Azariah and the Song of the Three Jews; Susanna; Bel and the Dragon; and 1–2 Maccabees. (These writings are known to Protestants as the Apocrypha or "hidden" books.) Orthodox Christians also accept these books as scriptural, along with a few others found in neither the Catholic nor Protestant canons.

Practices

Catholics celebrate several feast days in honor of the Blessed Virgin Mary. The principal ones are:

> **Assumption**. A feast celebrated August 15 commemorating the Assumption of Mary into heaven bodily.

> **Immaculate Conception**. A commemoration celebrated December 8 of the conception of Mary without original sin.

Because Latino Catholics now make up a significant segment of the United States Catholic population, mention should be made of religious holidays unique to them:

> **El Dia de los Reyes Magos** (the Day of the Magi Kings). Equivalent to the Feast of the Epiphany for other Christians (January 6), but for Latinos this is the day when gifts are exchanged (rather than Christmas).

> **El Dia de los Muertos** (the Day of the Dead). Celebrated November 2, this day is equivalent to All Souls' Day for other Christians.

> **Feast of Our Lady of Guadalupe**. Celebrated December 12, this is probably the most important of Latino Catholic holidays and a commemorates the appearance of the Virgin Mary to a Mexican Indian peasant, Juan Diego, in 1531.

> **Las Posadas** (the Wayside Inns). A commemoration of the difficulty Mary and Joseph had in journeying from Nazareth to Bethlehem and finding a place to stay prior to Jesus' birth. It is celebrated from December 16 to 24 with pageants, the lighting of candles, and the praying of the rosary (a devotional prayer to Mary using prayer beads).

Lent is a 40-day period during which Catholics abstain from meat on Ash Wednesday (the first day of Lent when ashes are rubbed on the foreheads of Catholics during mass as a sign of human mortality) and on all Fridays of Lent;

and they fast on Ash Wednesday and Good Friday. (Fasting for Catholics means eating only one full meal and two smaller ones.)

Catholics celebrate the Mass or Eucharist daily while most other Christians celebrate the Lord's Supper/Holy Communion/Eucharist weekly at most. Catholics are obliged to attend Mass only on Sundays and major holy days.

Although not as frequently as before the Second Vatican Council (1962–65), Catholics confess their sins privately to a priest in the sacrament of penance, or reconciliation. (They must do so at least once a year if they have sinned seriously and wish to receive Holy Communion.) The priest absolves them of the guilt involved, though not from possible future punishments in the afterlife in Purgatory (see below).

Catholics, like Orthodox Christians, accept the concept of Purgatory, a purifying experience in the afterlife for those who have lived a basically righteous life but have committed sins for which they must repent. The punishment or purgation consists of a painful longing for God for a period corresponding to the sins committed on earth.

Main Subgroups

There are no branches within Catholicism. A relatively small number of "Eastern rite" or "uniate" Catholics whose belief system is identical to those in the Roman system but whose celebration of the sacraments is slightly different, live in the United States. (In the countries of origin of these Eastern rites, such as Lebanon, priests may marry but not if they reside in the West.)

Common Misunderstandings and Stereotypes

"Catholics worship the Blessed Virgin Mary."

Though Catholics venerate Mary as the most important of the saints—and even pray to God through her—she is not considered divine but simply the holiest person, besides Jesus, who ever lived.

"Catholics accept the teachings of the pope as without error and the pope himself as incapable of sinning."

The pope is only considered as capable of teaching without error (infallibly) when he makes an official pronouncement on a matter of belief or morality in his official role as head of the church. Moreover, Catholics do not receive instructions from the pope or their bishops about whom to vote for, although the pope or the United States Conference of Bishops do publish statements instructing Catholics on matters of morality (abortion, euthanasia, etc.). The pope, although usually a person of high moral character, is just as capable of sinning as any other human being.

Classroom Concerns

On Ash Wednesday and the Fridays of Lent, nonmeat dishes should be available in the school cafeteria.

Anti-Catholic stereotypes about a Catholic's absolute allegiance to the pope or worship of Mary, which still persist to some degree, should be corrected if and when they are expressed by students.

Population Data

There are about 58 million Catholics in the United States (making Catholicism the largest single denomination or individual church in the country) and some 900 million worldwide.[1]

—B.H.

Notes

1. James A. Rudin, *A Jewish Guide to Interreligious Relations* (New York: American Jewish Committee, 1996), 53.

Further Reading

Bokenkotter, Thomas. *Essential Catholicism: Dynamics of Faith and Belief.* Garden City, NY: Doubleday, 1986.

Doyle, Dennis M. *The Church Emerging from Vatican II: A Popular Approach to Contemporary Catholicism.* Mystic, CT: Twenty-Third Publications, 1992.

McBrien, Richard P. *Catholicism, New Edition.* San Francisco: HarperCollins, 1994.

Christianity

Seventh-day Adventists

Origins

The Seventh-day Adventist Church grew out of the Great Disappointment, when the Millerite expectation of the return to Earth of Jesus Christ on October 22, 1844, did not take place. William Miller, a New England Baptist preacher, had based his calculations on the Bible, specifically the Book of Daniel. By the spring of 1845, Miller and most of his followers abandoned the time calculations concerning the Second Advent (Second Coming of Christ). A few retained their confidence in the time calculations, contending that Christ, instead of coming to Earth, had entered a new phase of ministry in the heavenly sanctuary. Some of the followers, including James and Ellen White, began keeping the seventh-day Sabbath. Mrs. White inspired the movement with her visions, prophecies, and writings, and she was influential in establishing educational, publishing, and medical missionary programs. The name Seventh-day Adventist Church was adopted in 1860 to distinguish the church from other Protestant churches and to highlight its missionary thrust.

Beliefs

Based on the Bible, especially the books of Daniel and Revelation, Seventh-day Adventists believe that their mission is to help prepare for the Second Coming of Christ by preaching the "everlasting gospel" to all the world as an antidote to increasing wickedness. When the Gospel has been effectively preached to all the world, Jesus Christ will return to Earth, resurrect the faithful dead (who are in a state of unconsciousness), grant them immortality, and take them back to heaven for the thousand-year reign of Christ, called the Millennium. This is the first resurrection. At this same time, Satan will be bound and cast into the bottomless pit. At the end of the Millennium, during the second resurrection, Satan will be released to deceive the nations, and all those who have died sinners will be raised. They will review their own roles in the history of the rebellion against God. They will confess that God is loving and just and that they do not want to exist under the conditions in his kingdom. God will cease sustaining their lives and they will cease to exist. Satan also will cease to exist. Then the Holy City, with all the saints, will return to earth, which will regain its original purity and become the eternal abode of the saints.

Christ's return will be very soon, although no exact date can be set. Still, current events can be read as signs of the times, revealing that the return is close at hand. In preparation for this event, all biblical principles must be restored. Because the Ten Commandments are central to Christ's high priestly ministry in the heavenly sanctuary, it is necessary that believers follow them. According to the Bible (Ex. 20:8–11), the fourth of the commandments is to keep the Sabbath day, Saturday. The Sabbath is a memorial of creation (for God rested on the seventh day, as human beings do). It is therefore a sign that, through faith, human beings will live righteously; and it is a sign of the coming new creation. Restoration of the Sabbath is necessary for Christ's return.

Sacred Books/Scriptures

The Bible alone is sacred and authoritative. Interpreting its message of the Second Advent of Christ is central to the church. The Bible predicts that the Second Advent will commence a thousand-year, or millennial, period. After the Great Disappointment, a reinterpretation of the Bible led to the principles that are central for Seventh-day Adventists today. Mrs. White's prophecies and writings are next in importance to the Bible in their spiritual authority.

Practices

The church operates as a representative democracy, with delegates meeting periodically to set policies regarding their missionary, educational, benevolence, health, and publishing activities. Local churches are independent and many operate their own schools. Pastors are trained in Adventist seminaries and assigned to local churches.

Adventists practice the ordinances of baptism by immersion (a symbol of conversion) and the Lord's Supper (preceded by foot washing); accept the gifts of prophecy; and treat the Bible as an infallible guide and rule for faith and practice.

In keeping with their view of the nearness of Christ's return to earth, Adventists do not conform to the world. They consider the body a temple of the Holy Spirit and avoid habits or practices that would defile it. They do not use alcohol, tobacco, or narcotics; avoid gambling and dancing; and observe proper decorum and modesty in dress. They are opposed to war, but prefer to serve as conscientious cooperators in the medical corps, rather than conscientious objectors.

In keeping with the emphasis on habits of health, they maintain hospitals and provide medical services, not only for Adventists but as a missionary outreach to non-Adventists as well. Mrs. White incorporated health reform into her theology and considered it an important dimension of religious experience. Healthful living is a part of the biblical principles to be restored before the return of Christ. Hence, health is a moral and spiritual virtue. It prepares one for that moment when the mortal body will be translated to immortality. Mrs. White also emphasized vegetarianism, in keeping with some of the mid-nineteenth-century health reform practices. The earth is to be restored to the perfect conditions of the Garden of Eden before the Fall; hence, Mrs. White reasoned that one ought to follow the practices of the first inhabitants, who ate only of the fruits, nuts, and grains that grew there. In addition, eating meat, which causes pain and death of animals, is the result of the Fall into sin and was not part of God's original plan.

Some Millerites discontinued evangelism after October 22, 1844, because they thought that, at that time, Christ had ceased his intercession for sinners, and therefore new conversions were impossible. At first, Sabbath-keeping Adventists adopted this view, but Mrs. White and others gradually modified the position through emphasizing the preaching needed to prepare for the Second Advent. Through their understanding of the importance of the Ten Commandments, and especially of the Sabbath, they stressed the need to tell all non-Adventists that the biblical principles, including the Sabbath, must be restored before Christ's return.

Main Subgroups

Some of the main subgroups are Branch SDAs; General Association of Davidian Seventh-day Adventists; People's Christian Church; The Registry; Seventh-day Adventists Church, Reform; Seventh-day Christian Conference; and Unification Association of Christian Sabbath Keepers.

Additionally, there are several Adventist groups in addition to Seventh-day Adventists: Jehovah's Witnesses; Advent Christian Church; Davidian Seventh-day Adventists Association; Church of God, International; General Conference of the Church of God; Worldwide Church of God; Assemblies of Yahweh; and a number of small, local groups.

Common Misunderstandings and Stereotypes

"Seventh-day Adventists are not Christian because they follow the Jewish practice of worshipping on Saturday."

It is true that there is a strong emphasis placed on the Hebrew Bible, especially the book of Daniel and the Ten Commandments. However, Adventists, like many other Christians, read and follow both the Old and New Testaments. By the second century, the Catholic Church had adopted the first day of the week, Sunday, as the chief day of worship, because it was on this day that Christ was raised from the dead. However, by giving priority to the authority of the Bible, and to the Ten Commandments in particular, Seventh-day Adventists became convinced of the need to return to the Sabbath, which they took as a sign of everlasting devotion between God and his worshippers.

"Seventh-day Adventists are not entirely consistent, expecting the imminent return of Christ but working to improve the world at the same time."

Following the Ten Commandments and observing the Sabbath are understood as expressions of faith in Jesus Christ. In addition, Mrs. White encouraged the establishment of hospitals and emphasized habits of healthy living (the church has a well-deserved reputation for its medical services). However, none of this contradicts the anticipation of Christ's imminent return. After the Great Disappointment, a reinterpretation of the Bible revealed that humanity was to be purified and true worship restored in preparation for the return. All members of the church are considered missionaries and are to contribute to a worldwide proclamation of this theme of restoration.

Classroom Concerns

Adventist students may want to be excused from school-related Saturday activities because this day is their Sabbath, and they are expected to participate in Adventist observances. Teachers might help these students organize their weekly schedule so that homework, for example, can be completed when they are not busy with church activities.

Some Adventist students follow a vegetarian diet. This is a religious practice, so provision should be made to accommodate their dietary requirements.

The Seventh-day Adventist view of history and the Sabbath may not be the same as other Christian or non-Christian views. For Adventists, their history is a sacred, true, and meaningful account of the world that includes an understanding of the nature of human life and its ultimate destiny as the Bible has foretold. If Adventist views are expressed in class, teachers might use the occasion to teach cultural diversity and toleration of different viewpoints.

Practices that set Adventists apart from the world, such as not eating meat and observing Saturday as the day of worship, should not be allowed to make Adventist children feel left out. When such practices are noticed by other students, teachers might use the occasion as an opportunity to develop a lesson on religious freedom, the exercise of conscience, and toleration of different beliefs.

Population Data

The *Seventh-day Adventist Yearbook*[1] lists worldwide membership at 8,609,055. Latin America, Africa, and Russia have experienced rapid membership gains in the past few years. The church operates 5,698 schools worldwide with 86 colleges and universities and 152 hospitals and sanitariums. There are about 825,000 Adventists in the United States.

—J.H.

Notes

1. Office of Archives and Statistics, General Conference of Seventh-day Adventists, *Seventh-day Adventist Yearbook* (Hagerstown, MD: Review and Herald Publishing, 1996).

Further Reading

Doan, Ruth Alden. *The Miller Heresy, Millennialism, and American Culture*. Philadelphia: Temple University Press, 1987.

Gaustad, Edwin, ed. *Rise of Adventism: Religion and Society in Mid-Nineteenth Century America*. New York: Harper & Row, 1974.

Numbers, Ronald L., and Jonathan M. Butler, eds. *The Disappointed: Millennialism in the Nineteenth Century*. Bloomington: Indiana University Press, 1987.

Spalding, Arthur W. *Origin and History of Seventh-day Adventists*. 4 vols. Washington, DC: Review & Herald Publishing, 1961.

Fundamentalism

Origins

There is no "Church of Fundamentalism" in the United States. Rather, there are Protestant churches that describe themselves as fundamentalist in orientation. Moreover, the term *fundamentalist* has been extended during the past 15 to 20 years (particularly since the Iranian revolution under the Ayatollah Khomeini in 1979) to include any follower of one of the world's religions who holds highly conservative views regarding his or her religion (e.g., forbidding unmarried adults of the opposite gender from having any contact unless accompanied by a chaperon).

The term *fundamentalism* was coined at the turn of the century when members of various Protestant denominations began to disagree over interpretation of the Bible. The more liberal among them accepted the scientific approach to interpreting the Bible, originating in Germany. The German biblical scholars used literary criticism, archeology, history, and other disciplines to interpret the meaning behind many "legendary" elements in the Hebrew and Christian Bibles (Old and New Testaments). Thus, for example, some of the miraculous events narrated in Exodus (the plagues upon the Egyptians, the parting of the Red Sea) or concerning Jesus' life (walking on water, multiplying loaves of bread and fish) were interpreted as symbolic rather than literally true.

By contrast, more conservative clergy and lay people objected to what they saw as an attempt to water down the word of God. From 1910 to 1915, a group of biblical scholars at Princeton Seminary and elsewhere published "The Fundamentals," a series of pamphlets that defended the literal truth of the Bible and cited specific doctrines contained in the scriptures that had to be accepted as fact to be of the Christian faith. These included Jesus' divinity and virgin birth, his death as the atonement for the sins of humankind, his bodily resurrection and physical return, his miracles, and the literal truth and reliability of every word of the Bible.

Beliefs

Christian fundamentalists accept the basic creeds and ethical codes of traditional Christianity but interpret them very conservatively. In particular, every word of the Bible is considered true and accurate, not only as regards religious aspects but historically and scientifically as well. For example, the accounts of creation and the flood in the opening chapters of Genesis are considered fact. Thus, God created the world about 10,000 years ago and did so directly and in this order: vegetation, fishes, birds, animals, insects, and finally humans. Evolutionary theories were expressly ruled out. Likewise, Noah literally took pairs of all animals into the ark during the deluge.

Opposition to evolution led to the 1923 Scopes "Monkey Trial" in which a young Tennessee biology teacher, John Scopes, was accused of teaching evolution in violation of Tennessee law. Though Scopes was found guilty, his conviction was later thrown out by the Tennessee Supreme Court. The net effect of the trial was ridicule of fundamentalists, causing them largely to avoid involvement in political affairs until the late 1970s. Then, the Rev. Jerry Falwell's Moral Majority was founded and—on the coattails of the Reagan presidency—entered the political world, particularly over issues such as abortion, creation science (a movement defending the Genesis creation accounts by criticizing the theory of evolution and providing its own scientific explanation of human origins), euthanasia, and prayer in school.

It is important to distinguish fundamentalists from evangelicals, a larger but more moderate grouping of conservative Christians (mainly Protestant) of some 50 to 60 million believers. (Though almost all fundamentalists are also evangelicals, the reverse is not true; *evangelical* is the more inclusive term for conservative Christians.) Although sharing a reverence for the Bible with fundamentalists, evangelicals are somewhat more open to interpreting the Bible and not quite as suspect of the secular world. Along with a centeredness in the Bible, the common threads of the two movements are (1) belief in the necessity of "believer's baptism," a mature commitment to Jesus Christ; and (2) dedication to evangelizing (converting others to Christianity).

The term *fundamentalism* has now been extended to include highly conservative— and sometimes fanatical—members of any religion. In this connection, the distinguished historian of religion Martin Marty[1] has created a profile of worldwide fundamentalism that includes the following characteristics:

1.   an "us versus them," extremist viewpoint that is unwilling to compromise with moderates within one's own faith and finds other religions completely lacking in truth;

2.   a defensive mentality that sees the outside world as massed against the true believers and trying to destroy them and their values, and that condemns certain nations or individuals (e.g., America as the "Great Satan" in the eyes of Iran's religious leaders and other Islamic fundamentalists);

3. a literal reading of scriptures allowing for interpretation only on the basis of other passages in the sacred text (Bible, Qur'an, etc.) and not on the basis of outside scholarly sources;

4. a missionary zeal that seeks to bring new recruits into the fold;

5. the desire to bring the state under the control of the fundamentalist religious community so that a theocracy—such as that in Iran—results;

6. a dominant role for men in all spheres of life so that the role of women is largely domestic;

7. a sense that the world is in a state of crisis or that "the end is near," and that the true believers will play a dominant role in the events of the end times; and

8. a sophisticated use of the tools, but not the values, of modernity—especially the media—in achieving its aims.

Sacred Books/Scriptures

Fundamentalists accept the sacred texts of their respective religions (Bible, Qur'an, etc.) but use them in an absolutist way, as indicated above.

Practices

Fundamentalists observe the same holidays and rituals as traditional believers. What differentiates the two groups is that fundamentalists may use a holiday as an occasion for a political protest demonstration (such as the attempts by the anti-abortion group Operation Rescue to block entry to reproductive health clinics during the week preceding Easter).

Main Subgroups

As noted in "Origins" above, fundamentalism is a philosophy operating within various religions and their subdivisions rather than a church unto itself. Thus, a significant portion of the country's 16 million Southern Baptists would consider themselves fundamentalists, as would many members of the Missouri and Wisconsin Synods (districts) of the Lutheran family of churches. One of the oldest Protestant centers of fundamentalism is Bob Jones University in South Carolina, which several years ago resisted federal efforts of forced racial integration, even at the cost of losing government funding.[2]

Common Misunderstandings and Stereotypes

"Fundamentalists are simply religious terrorists."

Though some fundamentalists have resorted to terrorism, as in the Middle East, most use nonviolent means to obtain their goals. In other words, a fundamentalist is not, by definition, a religious fanatic—someone who resorts to violent tactics to achieve goals. Examples of fanatical groups include: Haredi in Israel, which resorts to stone throwing on the Sabbath to prevent less religiously observant Jews from driving cars; HAMAS/Islamic Resistance Movement in the Palestinian territories, which has sent its members on suicide missions to kill Israelis; the Church of Jesus Christ Christian, Aryan Nations, which is closely associated with the Ku Klux Klan; and Sikh separatists who have used terror tactics in seeking to gain independence from India for Punjab State.

"Fundamentalists are ignoramuses or 'Bible thumpers.' "

One may not agree with the idea of taking the Bible literally to solve all of life's problems. However, many fundamentalists are educated people who simply feel that there is a source of wisdom higher than humanity—God's revealed word. They reason, moreover, that once you begin to tamper with or interpret the Bible or Qur'an, there is no end to the process. You ultimately end up, they believe, with a book of fairy tales.

Classroom Concerns

Fundamentalists may object to having their children exposed to units on world religions and have the right to remove them during such instruction and request alternate assignments. Halloween is considered by many fundamentalists a pagan holiday associated with witchcraft. Teachers might want to send a letter to parents to see how they feel about any activities planned for this holiday.

The teaching of evolution in biology/science classes presents problems for those families who reject it and espouse creation science (see "Beliefs" above). The Supreme Court ruled (*Edwards v. Aguillard*, 1987) that a Louisiana statute granting equal time to the teaching of creation science in science classes was unconstitutional. Creation science can, however, be discussed in world religions or social studies classes; and parents may remove their children from science classes when evolution is studied.

Sex education is another sensitive issue for conservative Christians, Jews, and Muslims. Some claim, for example, that information about birth control methods actually increases the incidence of teen pregnancy rather than preventing it. However, the State Court of Louisiana ruled in 1992 that Sex Respect, the sex education curriculum promoted by many conservative Christians, violated state law by promoting religious beliefs and disseminating inaccurate information. Here again, parents have the right to remove their children from programs they find objectionable. Discussions between parents and teachers may be helpful in clarifying a sex education curriculum.

A sensitive issue for some fundamentalist parents is the use of textbooks or other assigned readings found objectionable on various grounds: sexually explicit content, use of obscene language, allegedly pagan content, and so on. If a particular textbook has been problematic in the past, teachers might want to consult with parents about it.

Population Data

Kosmin and Lachman[3] estimate that there are about 17 to 20 million fundamentalist Christians in the United States. As far as we know, there has never been a scientific survey of the number of fundamentalists in other religions. However, it appears from press reports that there are significant numbers in Judaism, Islam, Hinduism, and Sikhism.

—B.H.

Notes

1. Martin E. Marty and R. Scott Appleby, eds., chap15, "Conclusion: An Interim Report on a Hypothetical Family." *Fundamentalism Observed* (Chicago: University of Chicago Press, 1991).

2. Members of Pentecostal churches (see the chapter "Protestantism"), though different from fundamentalists, who tend to be uncomfortable with such practices as speaking in tongues and the laying on of hands, share with fundamentalism literal interpretation of the Bible and use of evangelism.

3. Barry A. Kosmin and Seymour P. Lachman, *One Nation Under God: Religion in Contemporary American Society* (New York: Harmony Books, 1993), 197.

Further Reading

Lawrence, Bruce B. *Defenders of God: The Fundamentalist Revolt Against the Modern Age.* San Francisco: Harper & Row, 1989.

Martin, William. *With God on Our Side: The Rise of the Religious Right in America.* New York: Broadway Books, 1996.

The symbol of Hinduism is the sacred letter om (ohm) pronounced at the beginning and end of prayers and recitations from scripture. It is the seed of all mantras (sacred utterances).

Hinduism

Origins

Hinduism is generally considered to be the world's oldest continuing religion. It stems from several sources: aboriginal cultures; the Indus Valley culture (2500–1700 B.C.E.) and its possible descendants in south India belonging to the Dravidian language groups; and the Sanskrit-based Aryan culture and religion—Brahmanism—as contained in the Vedas or "Sacred Wisdom." The form of Hinduism familiar today first appeared around 500 B.C.E. with the composition of the epic literature, the Mahâbhârata and Râmâyana, and the later Purânas or "Ancient Stories."

By definition, Hinduism does not refer to one religion but rather to numerous religious movements, philosophies, teachings, and practices that originated in India over the course of thousands of years and are coextensive with the cultures of the Indian subcontinent. Indeed, the terms *Hindu* and *Hinduism* are artificial and overarching—etymologically identical with *India* and *Indian*—and attached to those religions that seem to be identified with the Indian world view. Although Buddhism, Jainism, and Sikhism are also Indian religions separate from Hinduism, it appears that this sense of separateness is more the choice of these religions than of Hinduism. Sikhism, for example, originated out of a branch of devotional Hinduism and was considered Hindu until the Sikhs themselves selected a separate identity.

Beliefs

What holds this web of philosophical and religious movements together as Hindu is the acceptance by most adherents of certain doctrines and practices that are either unique to, or closely identified with, Hinduism. Chief among these is the view that the scripture called the Vedas—especially the last part, the Upanishads—is the basis of all Hindu teaching and wisdom and is not of human origin. Two other compositions, the Mahâbhârata and Râmâyana, hold such great honor and prestige among the population that they probably have as much or more authority among most Hindus of all walks of life. Furthermore, other compositions possess a somewhat lesser position of authority because they are concerned with more specific departments of knowledge. An example of the latter are the Law Books (*dharma-sûtras* and *dharma-shâstras*), which define the manners and mores of the Hindu communities.

Other unifying factors are the celebration of a large number of festivals; the importance of pilgrimages to sacred sites for all Hindus; the acceptance of karma (any willed action produces an effect, good or bad, on the individual committing the action); belief in rebirth; the importance of the role of astrology in one's life; the presence of a large and bewildering number of divinities that are honored during certain festivals or in more private worship; the marriage ceremony as the most frequently performed of the life-cycle rituals; and caste or subsocieties that follow rules governing whom one may marry and eat with and, to a lesser extent, the occupation reserved for that group.

Sacred Books/Scriptures

The Vedas are the central scripture. It consists of more than 50 separate works divided into four sections: (1) collections of hymns: Samhitâs; (2) discussions of rituals and their contents: Brahmanas; (3) mystical discussions of selected rituals: âranyakas; and (4) "secret knowledge" of the nature of the supreme force both within and beyond the universe: Upanishads. While the first three sections are primarily concerned with attaining success in the world, the later portion of the Vedas—the Upanishads—is concerned with realizing the nature of the absolute and with attaining salvation from this world of ignorance.

Additionally, the two great epics, the Mahâbhârata (which includes the Bhagavad Gita; see "Main Subgroups" below) and the Râmâyana, have great popular appeal.

Practices

The main practices are festivals, pilgrimages, worship, and life-cycle rituals. Other practices that are commonly accepted are nonviolence (at least in principle), vegetarianism, and the veneration of the cow as a sacred creature.

Festivals include fasting, worship, feasting, dramatic spectacles, entertainment, dance, music, and sometimes a procession in which the divinity is paraded on a chariot through the streets. Celebrations are usually centered around national epics or stories of the divinities. Thousands of festivals are celebrated throughout India, but the following are more widely observed worldwide. (The dates of festivals vary from year to year because Hinduism follows a lunar calendar. The months begin around the 15th day of the solar months, with the year beginning in the month of Chaitra [March/April]. See Appendix B for a calendar.)

Dassehra (Dusserah). The festival lasting "ten days." This is perhaps the most popular of all festivals and is celebrated throughout the country for ten days in September/October. The first nine days are devoted to the worship of the goddess Durgâ in her nine guises; the 10th day is a celebration of the victory of Râma, hero of the Râmâyana, over Râvana, demon king of Sri Lanka.

Dîpâvali (Dîwâlî). The festival of lamps. This celebration honors Lakshmî, the goddess of wealth and good fortune, over a five-day period in September/October or October/November. It also commemorates Râma's victory over Râvana and Râma's return to the city of Ayodhyâ.

Sri Ramakrishna Jayanti. This celebration, in February, marks the birthday of the great nineteenth-century mystic, Sri Ramakrishna.

Shivarâtri (Night of Shiva). Celebrated throughout India in February/March by all Hindus, regardless of caste or class, it is at this time that Shiva manifests himself in the form of the flaming *linga* (the phallus, characteristic symbol of Shiva) to shower his grace on his devotees.

Holî. One of the most popular of Hindu festivals, this two-day spring festival celebrated in February/March marks the end of winter.

Râma-navamî. The birthday of Râma, celebrated in March/April.

Srî-Krishna-Jayantî. The birthday of Krishna, celebrated in July/August or August/September.

Pilgrimage to sacred sites such as cities or rivers is especially important not only for Hindus but also for Indians of other religions.

Worship (*pûjâ*) of a deity in human or abstract form or any object considered sacred is performed publicly and privately within the home. It may be a simple offering or a sequence of services, each one accompanied by a *mantra* or sacred sounds in the form of formulae, syllables, phrases, or hymns. The idea of a *pûjâ* is to honor the invited and invoked deity.

Life-cycle rituals include the birth ceremony, first feeding of the baby, giving of the baby's name, learning of the alphabet, initiation rite (the male child of the upper classes undergoes a spiritual rebirth and so becomes a twice-born), marriage and the funeral rite.

Main Subgroups

Traditionally, Hindus are grouped according to which deity is considered the chief divinity of devotion:

Shaiva Hindus worship Shiva as their main divinity, together with divinities associated with him, such as the consort of Shiva, Pârvatî; Gangâ, the deified Ganges River; the children of Shiva and Pârvatî: Ganesha and Skanda; and particular animals associated with Shiva: the cobra (*nâga*) and Nandi, the bull.

Vaishnava Hindus worship Vishnu or one of his incarnations. He is perhaps the most popular deity, especially in two earthly forms: (1) Krishna, who appears as the supreme lord-teacher of the popular scripture, the Bhagavad Gita; as the impish child who steals butter and slays demons and who subdued the serpent Kâliya as an adolescent; and as the paramour of the *gopîs* or cow-girls; and (2) Râma, the hero of the Râmâyana who defeats the demon king of Sri Lanka, Râvana; and husband to the ideal of Hindu womanhood, Sîtâ.

Many Hindus honor the Goddess (Devî) in one of her many manifestations representing the mother, life, and fertility. Sometimes referred to as **Shâkta Hindus**, one of the most popular manifestations is Durgâ, the slayer of the Buffalo-Demon. Other goddesses include Annapûrnâ, the beneficent goddess; Kâlî, the personification of the Goddess's anger; and Sarasvatî, the goddess of learning.

Many subdivisions of Hinduism also exist that follow the teachings of a great philosopher in the past, such as Shankara (788–820) or Râmânuja (1017–1137); or a leader of a devotional movement, such as Caitanya (1486–1533), the inspiration of the present-day Hare Krishnas; or a host of modern teachers or gurus, such as Sri Ramakrishna (1836–1886), the guru of Swami Vivekananda (Swami Vivekananda founded the Vedanta Society), and Aurobindo Ghose (1872–1950).

Common Misunderstandings and Stereotypes

What most non-Hindus know about Hinduism centers around certain popular misconceptions regarding cows, idol worship, rebirth, nonviolence, the caste system, and the almost incalculable number of divinities. Though based partly in fact, these misconceptions draw false conclusions and fail to recognize that Hindus are not unanimous in their own opinions of the above. Cows are venerated throughout India, but it is more a reflex or habit on the part of most Hindus, not conscious reflection. The cow is indeed venerated in some festivals such as Pongal, a festival held in southern India in January marking the end of the harvest season. The cow is extremely important because of its role in the agricultural areas of India and its close association with the earth.

Hindus use both anthropomorphic and abstract images of deities in worship, but this use is not idolatry in the strict sense. The image is not the object of worship but only the representative or container of the divinity during the period of worship. Many non-Hindus perceive Hindus to be nonviolent because of their notion of rebirth and suppose that, because a relative or family member can be reborn an animal or human, violence toward any animal or human might be directed at a former family member. Such opinions rarely arise among Hindus and are gross simplifications.

Caste does exist to this day, but many ideas about it were shaped from ancient writings or by generalizations no longer as prominent today. Although abuses exist, the attitudes towards caste are changing, especially in the cities such as Bombay, Calcutta, and New Delhi. Rural areas and villages, however, still retain some of the old conceptions of the hierarchical structure of caste. It is a complicated subject that defies generalization.

Finally, the number of gods is a problem for many who are acquainted with Hinduism. Throughout India, there are thousands of names associated with the divinities, but—despite this number—Hindus are not necessarily polytheists in the strict sense. According to philosophical background and sophistication, the acceptance of many divinities and the acceptance of one underlying ground of existence or force are not mutually exclusive. For many Hindus, the divine, whether personal or impersonal, may be accepted as supreme and absolute, and the other divinities— and for that matter the whole of creation—as being only manifestations of that supreme being.

Classroom Concerns

It is recommended that teachers and other professionals avoid making generalizations and judgments about Hinduism. This religion is represented by a large number of diverse practices and teachings that defy sweeping statements. Students with an Indian background most likely will come from families that perceive and understand Hinduism through a specific tradition of a particular teacher together with the practice of certain festivals, rites, and accompanying stories of the divinities honored in the festivals. Some students may know enough to comment on whatever appears in classroom texts and should be called upon to speak if they are comfortable with the situation. If not, parents or friends might be willing to give presentations on general aspects of Hinduism as they understand it. Such presentations lend an air of authenticity and are to be encouraged.

Population Data

Based on recent Indian census data, the population of Hindus is slightly more than 80 percent (600 million) of the total population of India. The total population of Hindus within the United States is about 650,000.[1]

—*J.S.*

Notes

1.   American population data of Hindus are based on immigration data giving the number of Indians who have entered the United States, especially since 1965. Indian data are based on the 1991 *Census of India* and *India Paper of 1995: Religion*, compiled by Dr. M. Vijayanunni, Census Commissioner, India.

Further Reading

Basham, A. L. *The Wonder That Was India.* New York: Grove Press, 1954.

Miller, Barbara Stoler, trans. *The Bhagavad-Gita.* Toronto: Bantam, 1986.

Mitchell, A. G. *Hindu Gods and Goddesses.* London: Her Majesty's Stationery Office, 1982.

Santucci, James. *Hindu Art in South and Southeast Asia.* Self-published. Fullerton: California State University, 1987.

The crescent moon and star symbolize the beginning of Ramadan, the Muslim month of fasting, which is determined by a sighting of the crescent. Originally, this symbol was a sociocultural representation of the fertile crescent between the Tigris and Euphrates Rivers. Only later did it take on religious significance.

Islam

Origins

Islam (meaning "peace through total submission to God's will") began with a series of divine revelations to prophet Muhammad in about 610 C.E. in which he received his mission to bring belief in one God (monotheism) to the people of Arabia and humankind generally. However, the religion received its greatest impetus through the Hijrah [HEEJ-rah] in 622 C.E. (the year 0 in the Muslim calendar) when Muhammad was forced to flee from Makkah (Mecca) in the Arabian peninsula to Medina, where he established the first Muslim community.

Beliefs

Muslims are monotheists who accept the same God as Jews and Christians but call the deity Allah [al-LAH] (Arabic for "the God"). They revere the same biblical figures, including Noah, Abraham, and Moses. Jesus is also considered a prophet but not the divine son of God, and Muhammad is the final prophet. Hence, the Muslim declaration of faith (creed) simply states: "There is no deity except Allah and Muhammad is his messenger." Muslims believe in an afterlife of rewards or punishments.

Sacred Books/Scriptures

The Qur'an [kur-AHN] (less accurately spelled Koran) is the sole scripture of Islam. The Old Testament and New Testament are respected as earlier revelations from Allah, but errors and loss of material have rendered them less accurate over time. Consequently, they are not considered equal to the Qur'an, which is understood by Muslims as "setting the record straight" on particular points. It is the literal word of God revealed to Muhammad from age 40 through the remaining 23 years of his life. He memorized the revelations and dictated them to various disciples, who also memorized and, in some cases, wrote them down. A few years later, Zaid ibn Thabit collected this material into what is now known as the Qur'an. The scripture, written in Arabic, consists of a series of 114 chapters (suras) arranged roughly in descending order of length.

Practices

The Muslim way of life rests on the Five Pillars: the creed "There is no deity except Allah and Muhammad is his messenger"; prayer five times daily (at dawn, noon, afternoon, sunset, and night); fasting from dawn until sunset during the month of Ramadan (no food, drink, or sexual relations); charitable giving (generally reckoned at 2.5 percent of one's savings); and a one-time pilgrimage (*Hajj*) to Makkah, Islam's holiest city, by all who are physically and financially able. The exact implementation of the pillars and other practices is dictated by the Sunnah [SOON-uh], the collected words and deeds of the prophet Muhammad. For example, the Qur'an mandates that Muslims pray daily, while the Sunnah instructs one on the exact times and manner of praying.

The Muslim day of communal worship is Friday, when Muslim men are required to gather at noon in the mosque (*masjid*) for prayer and a sermon by the imam [ee-MOM] or prayer leader. (Women may also attend but are not obliged to do so.) Friday is not a day of rest in the Jewish or Christian sense, but some Muslims may take the day off—or part of it—where possible.

Muslims observe two holidays:

'Id al-Fitr [ayd all-FAI-tur] (Festival of Fast-Breaking). The lesser of the two holidays, 'Id al-Fitr occurs at the close of the Ramadan fast and is a time of feasting and gift giving.

'Id al-Adha [ayd all-a-DAH] (Festival of Sacrifice). 'Id al-Adha occurs on the 10th day of the month when pilgrimages are made to Makkah. Besides being a festive time, 'Id al-Adha is a period of sacrifice commemorating the prophet Abraham's willingness to offer up his son Ishmael. Because Allah provided Abraham a ram instead, Muslims sacrifice an animal as part of the rites of the *Hajj* (pilgrimage) and give away one-third to needy families and one-third to friends.

Because Muslims use a lunar calendar that is about 11 days shorter than the solar cycle, the solar date of Muslim holidays—and the month of Ramadan—move through the seasons in a 32-year cycle. The calendar of religious holidays in Appendix B should be consulted when school events, for example, are being scheduled. Note that the majority of Muslims rely on the actual sighting of the new crescent moon on day 29 of Ramadan to determine when the month of fasting has ended. If it is not sighted because of weather conditions, the fast is continued for one more day. The date of 'Id al-Fitr as listed in Appendix B could possibly be one day premature. Further, all Muslim days begin at sundown (as in Judaism). Thus, when a non-Muslim calendar shows that a Muslim holiday begins on a particular day, be aware that it actually starts the evening before.

Muslims are forbidden to eat pork or pork derivatives, and meat must be slaughtered according to Islamic law. (Muslims in the West often eat Jewish kosher foods to be sure that no pork is present.) However, Muslims are permitted to eat in the homes of others "who have received the Scripture" (Qur'an, sura 5:5)—Jews and Christians—without worrying about the status of the food. Muslims must also refrain from consuming alcohol and other intoxicating substances.

Circumcision of male children is required, but female circumcision is neither required nor approved.

Main Subgroups

Sunni. About 85 to 90 percent of Muslims worldwide belong to this branch of the faith (Sunnah in Arabic means "customary practice," i.e., the practice of the prophet Muhammad). Sunni Muslims rejected the notion that the prophet Muhammad's blood-descendants should inherit his authority and opted instead for the election of their leader, or caliph.

Shi'a (or Shi'i). The smaller branch derives its name from *Shi'a Ali*, the party of Ali, the prophet Muhammad's cousin and son-in-law. Shi'a Muslims venerate a series of Ali's descendants as imams, or revered leaders, the last of whom will return at the end of time to redeem the world. Shi'ism also holds that the Qur'an contains hidden meanings that refer to Ali. Iran, Iraq, Bahrain, and Azerbayjan are the countries where Shi'a Muslims constitute the majority.

Sufism. Not a branch as such, Sufism is a mystical movement within Islam dating from the eighth century which stresses Allah's immanence and the possibility of mystical union with him. It is best known through the "Whirling Dervishes" only prominent in Turkey but suppressed in 1925 by Turkish ruler Ataturk. Small Sufi communities now exist in North America.

In the United States, where Muslims are a minority religion, rivalry between these two branches is minimal and one's identity as a Muslim is foremost. Hence, intermarriage between a Sunni Muslim and a Shi'a Muslim is not problematic, as it is in some predominantly Islamic countries.

Although as many as 1 million African Americans are Muslim, Louis Farrakhan's Nation of Islam is not considered a legitimate Islamic group by United States Muslim authorities. Still, the Nation of Islam's members follow most Muslim practices, such as the Five Pillars. They do not, however, accept the Muslim belief that people of all colors and ethnicities are equal in God's sight and thus may belong to Islam.

Common Misunderstandings and Stereotypes

"This religion is called 'Muhammadanism.' "

Although this term is still found in some older books, it is completely inaccurate. Muhammad was not a divine being but simply God's last and greatest prophet. Muslims stress the idea that the religion consists of submission to God, not Muhammad. Islam is the name of the religion, and Muslim (more accurate phonetically than Moslem) is the name for one who submits to the religion.

"Islam is a militaristic religion."

This idea springs in part from an oversimplified reading of history in which Islam is viewed to have spread initially by armed force. In fact, people accepted Islam freely, consistent with the saying in the Qur'an that "there shall be no compulsion in religion" (sura 2:256). The charge of militarism also stems from a misunderstanding of the term *jihad*. It does mean "military struggle in defense of Islam," and some of Islam's principles for defensive warfare anticipated the current Geneva Accords on this issue. Another meaning is "spiritual struggle or striving to become a better Muslim." However, it does not mean "holy war." Occasional acts of terrorism by a minority of Muslims—especially in connection with the quest for Palestinian self-determination—have also caused some people to label all Muslims as fanatics or terrorists.

"Muslims are prudish and puritanical."

Although Islam stresses modesty and prohibits the use of alcohol, sexual love in marriage is considered a great blessing from God. Ironically, earlier Western views of Islam stressed its male licentiousness, as exemplified by Muhammad's having been married to several women (though only after his first wife Khadija had died) and the practice of polygamy (see below). This, too, is a caricature.

"Islam is a religion that suppresses women."

Most of the criticisms of Islam in this respect stem from local customs or practices in particular countries or regions and have no basis in Islamic doctrine. For example, Islam does not condone female circumcision, which predates the religion and is most widely practiced in sub-Saharan Africa where educated Muslims are trying to eliminate it. On the positive side, a woman after marriage retains whatever property or possessions she owns; has full rights over her property (to buy, sell, etc.) and wage earnings; and has specific inheritance rights guaranteed by the Qur'an. It is true that a woman may not serve as imam or prayer leader, but this prohibition parallels the refusal of Orthodox Judaism and Roman Catholicism to ordain women as clergy. Finally, a word about polygamy: it is permitted, but not encouraged. A man may marry up to four wives, but only if he can financially and emotionally support each wife, with equality—no small task.

Classroom Concerns

Teachers should familiarize themselves with the dates of the two principal Muslim holidays, 'Id al-Fitr and 'Id al-Adha, and with the Ramadan fast (see "Practices" above) and make allowances for students who must be absent from school (and, in the case of physical education classes, for those who are fasting). Teachers should also try to be sensitive to students who need to do their required prayer while at school.

Because Islam generally prohibits art that represents a human being, it is recommended that teachers be sure alternative assignments are provided in art classes. More importantly, though, teachers should discuss the matter with the student, because many Muslim authorities permit depiction under certain circumstances (e.g., anatomy diagrams, instructional illustrations, and figurative toys for children).

Islamic rules of modesty may require that Muslim students wear sweat pants (at least to the knees) and long-sleeved T-shirts in physical education classes. It is recommended that teachers permit this even if other students are wearing gym shorts. Also, some Muslim girls may wear a head covering (*hijab*), a symbol of modesty, in school. To avoid leaving such students open to ridicule, teachers might want to explain these customs to other students in the class.

Male and female students might wish to be seated among same-sex members of the class and should be given this option. Similarly, dating, mixed-sex dancing, and other forms of premarital intimacy are not permitted in Islam. Consequently, it is suggested that Muslim students not be urged to attend proms and other social activities that bring boys and girls together.

Because Muslims are not comfortable with some of the practices surrounding Halloween and Valentine's Day, care should be taken that they not be required to participate in classroom projects related to these days.

Population Data

There are an estimated 1 billion Muslims worldwide, with large concentrations in the Arab world, Iran, Pakistan, and Indonesia. There are about 5 million Muslims in the United States.[1]

—B.H.

Notes

1. Robert Famighetti, ed. *World Almanac and Book of Facts* (New York: World Almanac Books/Funk & Wagnalls, 1997), 646.

Further Reading

Denny, Frederick M. *An Introduction to Islam.* New York: Macmillan, 1985.

Esposito, John L. *Islam: The Straight Path.* New York: Oxford University Press, 1991.

Schimmel, Annemarie. *Islam—An Introduction.* Albany, NY: State University of New York Press, 1992.

The symbol of Jainism is that of a wheel on the palm of the hand. The wheel has 24 spokes representing the 24 Great Teachers in the Jain tradition; the five fingers of the hand represent the five Great Vows, and within the central portion of the wheel is the word ahimsâ (nonviolence) (not shown in this version of the symbol).

Jainism

Origins

From an historical perspective, the religion known as Jainism [JAI-nism] was most probably established by Mahâvîra, "Great Hero" (so called because he stands fast in the midst of dangers and fears, and bears up under all hardships). An older contemporary of the Buddha, Vardhamâna Mahâvîra was most likely born in 599 or 598 B.C.E. (dates vary) and died around 527 or 526 B.C.E. In Jain tradition, however, Mahâvîra was but the last of a long line of 24 Great Teachers known as Tîrthankaras [Teer-TUN-karas] (Ford-makers), who reestablished the ancient spiritual path and truth. Of these 24, the only other likely historical figure who may have had a hand in establishing a Jain movement was the previous Great Teacher, Pârshvanâtha (872 or 817–772 B.C.E.).

The name of the religion reflects the nature of the founders: Jain refers to a follower of a *jina*, or spiritual victor. All the Great Teachers are *jinas* by virtue of the fact that they have acquired supreme knowledge and have overcome all inner imperfections, such as greed and anger. They are Tîrthankaras because they provided the means by which suffering can be conquered. In other words, a Tîrthankara is a teacher of salvation.

The life of Mahâvîra (and Pârshvanâtha) follows the pattern of the religious hero and, not unlike the life of the Buddha, includes miracles and marvels. Born in the northern Indian state of Bihar and raised in a family of the second class of society (administrators, rulers, and protectors), he spent his first 30 years living among householders (who, coincidentally, were followers of Pârshvanâtha). He married Yashodâ at 16 and had a daughter (one sect of Jains, the Digambaras, deny both his marriage and fatherhood). Like the Buddha, Mahâvîra lived in a palace surrounded by opulence. At the age of 30, he received permission from his elder brother and other authorities to leave the palace, his family, and possessions. He went to a park near his hometown, removed his ornaments, pulled out his hair in five handfuls, fasted for two and one-half days, and put on the robes of an ascetic (practitioner of penance) for a year. He then renounced clothing and entered the homeless, wandering life of a renunciant. After a period of 12 years of wandering, meditating, and fasting for long periods of time, he attained "complete, perfect or infinite knowledge," becoming omniscient. He thus knew completely the affairs of all living beings in the world and the previous and future births of gods, humans, animals, and demons. As a Tîrthankara for the next 30 years, he became a wandering teacher attracting disciples from all walks of life, eventually organizing a community into a fourfold order consisting of monks, nuns, laymen, and laywomen. At age 72, after giving a 48-hour sermon to his followers, he died in the city of Pâvâ (some 250 years after the liberation of Pârshvanâtha, according to tradition).

Beliefs

The goal of the Jain is the liberation of the soul from the bondage of this world of suffering, ignorance, pain, and rebirth. What causes bondage and rebirth is *karma* (action), so ultimately all action must be abandoned. Inherently connected to this goal is *ahimsâ* (nonviolence), which is the very basis of Jainism. No living being is to be harmed, injured, oppressed, enslaved, or killed—including microorganisms, plants, insects, animals, and humans. Realistically, this goal can only be approximated by the ascetic and homeless monks and nuns, not by the lay community.

In addition, non-attachment to materiality is also important to the Jain practitioner. It is, therefore, to be expected that Jainism is a religion that is ideally practiced by ascetics, not by the lay community. At the inception of the religion, the attitude persisted that the lay people could not help but perform violent actions or be attached to worldly things because of the needs of survival in this world. This attitude, however, has changed considerably over the millennia with the recognition that ascetics were dependent upon lay support. Therefore, a place was found for the participation of lay people in Jain practice, although the ascetic life is still the ideal.

Jainism today stresses religious tolerance, purity of action, and proper religious attitude. These are reflected in the Three Jewels of the religion: (1) Right insight allows one to see reality according to its true nature. (2) Right knowledge involves the intellectual understanding of the insight. (3) Right conduct is the action necessary to realize this insight.

Liberation or freedom is achieved when all actions (*karma*) are destroyed. *Karma* itself refers not only to actions and their results but also to material residue that associates itself with the soul. There are many varieties of *karma*: Some karmic actions can be destroyed by the knowledge and practice revealed by Mahâvîra and the Great Teachers who came before him. Some karmic actions cannot be altered by practice or knowledge. One's gender, length of life, species (human or nonhuman), family, and personality, for instance, are all determined by past *karma*s. However, if a person is liberated, there will be no return to this or any other world of suffering. The soul will then rise to the top of the universe, where only liberated souls reside, beyond the lower, earthly and heavenly worlds of the unliberated. Those souls not liberated will be reborn in a body (human or nonhuman) and location appropriate to the *karma* performed in their previous lives.

Sacred Books/Scriptures

The Jain canon formerly consisted of about 60 books, divided into three sections. The first section, known as the *Pûrva* ("Previous" or "Ancient"), consisted of 14 texts that supposedly date back to the time of Pârshvanâtha. Although lost, the subject matter is listed in later works. Subjects such as astrology and methods of attaining occult and psychic powers were included in the *Pûrva* texts.

The other two sections of the canon that comprise the present canon are the *Angas* ("Limbs")—12 in number though the last work, the *Drishtivâda*, is lost—and the *Angabâhya* ("Outer Limb"), which in turn is subdivided into the 12 *Upânga* ("Subsidiary Limbs"); the seven (one of which is lost) *Cheda-sûtras* ("Aphorisms or Scriptures on the Reduction of a Monk's Seniority," in other words, monastic discipline); the four *Mulasûtras* ("Root Scriptures"); the ten *Prakîrnaka-sûtras* ("Mixed or Miscellaneous Scriptures"); and the *Cûlikâ-sûtras* ("Appendix").

The 45 texts comprise the canon for most Shvetâmbara [shvay-TUM-ba-ra] Jains, more specifically, the Image Worshipping Assembly (see "Main Subgroups" below), as opposed to the aniconic (image-denying) subgroups within the Shvetâmbara community: the Sthânakavâsîs and Terâpanthîs, who recognize a 32-book canon. The other major division of Jainism, the Digambara [di-GUM-ba-ra], recognize the names of the Pûrva and Anga texts but assert that these texts have not survived in their original form. Topics that appear in these texts of the Shvetâmbara canon include monastic discipline, doctrinal issues, a discussion of non-Jaina teachings, mythology, cosmology, and biographies of those who are reborn as gods and who transcended rebirth altogether.

Practices

Jainism stresses practice rather than doctrine. It is not surprising, therefore, to find a multitude of practices for ascetics and lay persons. Both must follow five practices, known as Great Vows for ascetics, Restricted Vows for lay persons. The only distinction between the two is the degree of stringency of practice, with the demands on the ascetics much greater. The five vows are (1) abstention from violence (for ascetics, it is total; for lay persons, it is recognized that violence or injury does occur through no fault of the lay person); (2) abstention from lying; (3) abstention from taking what is not given; (4) abstention from sexual activity (for ascetics, it is complete chastity; for lay persons, any sexual activity outside of marriage); and (5) abstention from attachment. Besides these, an additional seven vows are undertaken by lay persons—three Subsidiary Vows and four Vows of Instruction. Subsidiary Vows, which expand upon the Restricted Vows, include: (1) restriction of travel; (2) restriction from certain foods (such as garlic, carrots, and ginger); and (3) restriction from certain activities that might be harmful (gambling or any activity that might promote violence). The four Vows of Instruction include: (1) meditation (to achieve a state of equanimity), (2) further restrictions on travel, (3) fasting on certain days of the month, and (4) charity.

In addition, there are certain food restrictions that are almost universally practiced: not eating meat, figs, or honey, nor partaking in alcohol. Vegetarianism, therefore, is strictly practiced, involving abstinence from not only meat, eggs, milk products, and fish, but also certain fruits and vegetables, such as onions, garlic, and fruit with lots of seeds. Onions and garlic are included under their notion of meat, since they are believed to possess life forms (perhaps due to their shape), as does the above-mentioned fruit.

Both ascetics and lay persons may also practice a "religious death," the practice of fasting and meditation that will gradually lead to one's demise. The practice is rare, however.

Ascetics, of which only a small proportion make up the total Jain population, practice total renunciation. Central to all Jain practice, lay and ascetic, is nonviolence. With this in mind, any activity that might cause violence is avoided, including a number of activities that seem innocent enough: bathing, fanning oneself, walking on greenery or touching a living plant, and digging. All can be harmful to living organisms. Shvetâmbara Jain monks wear a mouth shield to filter out microorganisms. All ascetics undergo an initiation that symbolizes a spiritual rebirth. The male initiate then takes on the lineage name of his teacher, renounces all clothing if he is a Digambara ascetic (nuns are not allowed to go naked), takes the three robes if he is a Shvetâmbara ascetic, and wears a mouth shield if the male or female ascetic is a Sthânikavâsî or Terâpanthî. In addition to undertaking the five Great Vows, ascetics undertake certain "essential duties," which are also recommended for the laity: a form of meditation or spiritual activity known as "equanimity," praise of the 24 Great Teachers, homage to the ascetic's teacher, repentance, abandonment of the body (assuming a motionless position, standing or sitting), and abandonment of certain foods or activities.

Worship directed toward a Great Teacher or Tîrthankara is also performed in the temple, which includes walking around the image of the Tîrthankara three times, sprinkling and drying the image, offering eight substances (water, sandalwood paste, flowers, incense, a lamp, uncooked rice, sweets, fruits), reciting the names of the 24 Tîrthankaras, and performing the waving of lamps before the image.

Certain holidays are considered very significant, such as the anniversary of Mahâvîra's birth (April/May) and death (or final liberation) (October/November). An important event, the Paryushana Parva, takes place in August/September. For a period of eight or ten days (for Shvetâmbaras and Digambaras respectively), lay persons fast; worship Mahâvîra; listen to a recitation of his biography; and, in the concluding portion of the event, make known their sins, ask for forgiveness, and extend their own forgiveness to all. Three other holidays are shared by Jains and Hindus: Rakhi (celebration of love and friendship; August); Dusserah (celebration of good over evil; October/November); and Dîwâlî (festival of lights; October/November).

Main Subgroups

Jains are divided into two major divisions or traditions: the Shvetâmbara and Digambara. The differences between the Shvetâmbara and Digambara Jains is primarily one of outward appearance and ascetic practice, which are regarded as an index to the proper understanding of the doctrine. One important difference is that Digambara male ascetics practice nudity; Shvetâmbara ascetics do not. Another is that Digambara ascetics do not use bowls for eating (only cupped hands), whereas Shvetâmbara ascetics do.

Besides these differences, there are important differences regarding the status of women. Women were allowed to enter mendicant (begging) orders, but Digambaras place female ascetics on a lower level than male ascetics because they are not to go naked. Shvetâmbaras, however, place women on a more equal level, but women ascetics are required to pay homage to even a newly initiated monk. Women cannot reach the same level of omniscience as men in the Digambara opinion, whereas the Shvetâmbaras accept women as capable of achieving omniscience.

Another important difference is the interpretation of the Great Teachers (*jinas* or "spiritual victors"). Digambaras consider them to be omniscient, therefore devoid of sensual perception and in constant meditation. A *jina*, therefore, communicates the teachings not through the voice or by example but through means of the "divine sound." It is supposedly understood by his audience and converted to scriptural tracts by his disciples. Shvetâmbaras, however, believe that the *jinas* can be both omniscient and engage in human activities.

One final difference concerns the scriptures. Digambaras reject Shvetâmbara scriptures.

Common Misunderstandings and Stereotypes

Jainism is not well known in the United States, but pockets of Jainism are developing in major metropolitan areas. What little is known about the religion is its strict adherence to nonviolence (familiar to Americans through the Rev. Martin Luther King Jr.'s teaching and practice) and vegetarianism. A misconception that might arise is the degree of adherence to these practices. Lay persons are not expected to be as strict in these practices as ascetics.

"Total nonviolence is unrealistic."
Jains look at the outside world with its incessant violence causing death and destruction and ask how unrealistic their world view really is.

Classroom Concerns

The Jain adherence to nonviolence and strict vegetarianism might present some problems for teachers and school administrators. Any action that is perceived as violent is ideally to be avoided by a Jain student. Dissection in biology classes presents an obvious problem. Contact sports in gym classes may also not be appropriate for the student. Discussion of violent events in history (wars, for instance) may not be viewed in the same light as that expressed in textbooks or in the classroom, especially if the war is glorified. It is recommended that teachers speak to the parents of the student should a problem arise. Vegetarian lunch choices should always be available for Jain children.

Population Data

Jainism is a small religion when compared to other traditional faiths. In India, the total Jain population is 3.4 million, according to the 1991 *Census of India*—smaller than the Christian, Sikh, and Buddhist populations. Worldwide, the Jain population is close to 4 million. There are 75,000 Jains in the United States and Canada, with more than 60,000 in the United States alone.

—J.S.

Further Reading

Dundas, Paul. *The Jains.* London and New York: Routledge, 1992.

Jaini, Padmanabh S. *The Jaina Path of Purification.* Delhi: Motilal Banarsidass Publishers, 1979.

The Star of David ("Shield of David" in Hebrew) probably had no historical connection to King David, and its origins are uncertain. It became a Jewish symbol in the 1600s in Prague, where it appeared on the official seal of the community and in prayer books. In 1897 it became the seal of the First Zionist Congress, and in 1948 was made the central emblem on the flag of new State of Israel.

Judaism

Origins

The Jewish people originated with the patriarch Abraham in about 1800 B.C.E. Judaism as a religious system began about 1250 B.C.E. with Moses, whom God commanded to lead the Hebrew slaves out of Egypt and with whom God established a covenant or pact on Mt. Sinai. Though the ancient Israelites had their own God (whose sacred name was Yahweh—a name Jews do not pronounce for fear of using it disrespectfully), strict monotheism did not develop until after the Babylonian exile of the Jewish nation in 538 B.C.E.

Beliefs

Judaism centers on belief in one God (monotheism) who chose the Jews to carry on an ethical and religious lifestyle spelled out in the Torah (the first five books of the Bible). A traditional summation of Jewish belief is to imagine the Jewish people, the Torah, and the land of Israel (promised land) as three points on a triangle with God at the center. Judaism has no elaborate creed (like Christianity, for example), but instead stresses the observance of the commandments in the Torah and, more generally, the living of an ethical life.

The essence of Jewish faith is perhaps best expressed in the words of Deuteronomy 6:4 (known in Hebrew as the *Sh'ma*): "Hear, O Israel, the Lord is your God, the Lord alone." It is said at every Jewish Sabbath service.

97

Although more traditional Jews do believe in an afterlife of rewards and punishments, Jews generally—unlike Christians and Muslims—do not emphasize the idea. In fact, more liberal Jews are quite agnostic on the point and hardly discuss it. Life is to be lived here and now for its own sake. Thus, the familiar expression *L'Haim,* "To life!"

Sacred Books/Scriptures

The Hebrew Bible (so named because it is written almost entirely in the Hebrew language) consists of three parts: the Torah (the law), the Prophets (Joshua, Isaiah, Jeremiah, etc.), and the Writings (Psalms, Proverbs, the Book of Job, etc.). Its contents are the same as what Christians call the Old Testament. Jews do not call it that because this would imply acceptance of the New Testament, which is exclusive to Christianity.

In addition to the Bible, Jewish life over the centuries has been profoundly influenced by the Talmud, an interpretation of the 613 laws found in the Torah (Genesis, Exodus, Leviticus, Numbers, and Deuteronomy). The Talmud is a vast and complex document. It both explains precisely how various commandments, such as hallowing the Sabbath, are to be observed; and presents stories about famous early rabbis, medical lore, and other material about living according to Jewish tradition.

Practices

Some Jews "keep kosher" by following a dietary code that permits only certain foods to be eaten (no pork products, shellfish, or meat-eating animals, for example). Meat must come from a kosher market (ensuring that the animal has been correctly slaughtered and all its blood removed). Also, meat and dairy products may not be eaten at the same meal. Jews who follow this system do not eat in the homes of friends who do not keep kosher, or in non-kosher restaurants.

Orthodox Jewish males wear a *yarmulke* [YAR-mul-keh], a small head covering that signifies respect for the presence of God, and an undershirt with tassels that serves as a constant reminder of the commandments one must observe.

Jewish males are circumcised on the eighth day after birth as a sign of the covenant with God. The ritual is performed by a specially trained individual, a *mohel* [MOY-el]. A baby-naming ceremony for girls is now common among more liberal Jews.

The ceremony of entry into adult Jewish life is the *Bar* (son) or *Bat* (daughter) *Mitzvah* (of the commandment). Boys at age 13 and girls at 12 or 13 conduct a synagogue service, read part of that week's portion from the Torah in Hebrew, and address the community. A celebration follows the service, and it is customary for guests to bring a gift. Anything an ordinary teenager would like is appropriate, or religious items may be given.

The Sabbath, the most important holiday, lasts from sundown on Friday until one hour after sundown on Saturday. A festive meal ushers in this holiday. Many Jews refrain from workaday activities (including, in the case of Orthodox Jews, driving a car and using the telephone) on the Sabbath. Jews attend synagogue services, led by a rabbi, either on Friday evening or Saturday morning.

Among the other Jewish holidays—all of which are on a lunar calendar and thus movable—four have the most effect on the lives of American Jews:

Rosh HaShanah [Rosh Ha-SHAN-ah] (The Jewish New Year). A time of rejoicing, but this holiday initiates a 10-day period of reflection on how well one has lived during the year just ended. Celebrated in September/October.

Yom Kippur [Yom kee-PUUR] (The Day of Atonement). This holiday is celebrated 10 days after the New Year. Jews fast for 25 hours from all food and drink and spend time in prayer and reflection.

Hanukkah [HA-nu-kah]. The Festival of Lights, celebrated in December and lasting for eight days, commemorates the Jerusalem Temple's re-dedication in 165 B.C.E. after a severe religious persecution. Each evening, candles are lighted in the home to commemorate the legend that the temple sanctuary light, after being rekindled, miraculously kept burning for eight days even though having enough oil for only one day. More important than the legend is that the light of Judaism, threatened with extinction, kept glowing because of the heroism of Jews who refused to forsake their faith.

Passover. This March/April holiday commemorates the Hebrews' Exodus or escape from Egypt and consists of an elaborate meal known as the *Seder* [SAY-der], in the home. No food containing yeast may be eaten during the eight days of Passover.

All Jewish holidays begin at sundown. Consequently, when a secular calendar gives a particular date as the start of a holiday, be aware that it actually begins the evening before. Most Jews will not go to work or school on the Jewish New Year and Day of Atonement. Orthodox and Conservative Jews will do the same on the day after the New Year, the first two and last two days of the eight-day Passover festival, and on two other holidays: Sukkot (the Feast of Tabernacles), in September/October, and Shavuot (the Feast of Weeks), in May/June.

Main Subgroups

Orthodox. The most traditional Jews, the Orthodox, adhere strictly to the interpretation of Jewish life contained in the Talmud (see "Sacred Books/Scriptures" above). They comprise about 7 percent of practicing Jews in the United States.[1] In a notable subgroup of Orthodoxy, Hasidic Jews, males dress in black suits and hats and wear beards.

Conservative. Though quite observant in areas such as keeping the Sabbath and the dietary laws, Conservative Jews are more willing than Orthodox to reinterpret talmudic traditions to correspond with changed modern conditions. They will, for example, drive to the synagogue on Saturday for services. They comprise about 38 percent of practicing Jews in the United States.

Reconstructionist. A recent offshoot of the Conservative movement, Reconstructionism stresses Judaism as a civilization or culture, rather than simply a religion, and rejects the notion of Jews as a chosen people. Less then 2 percent of practicing Jews are Reconstructionist, though the movement is growing.

Reform. The Reform branch is the most liberal and does not require such traditional practices as keeping kosher or strictly observing the Sabbath. Reform practice is based on the premise that the Bible is of human origin, so that each individual must decide what God wants of him or her. The movement stresses ethical conduct as the centerpiece of religion. Of practicing Jews in the United States, about 43 percent are Reform.

A note about Jews for Jesus, Messianic Jews, Hebrew Christians, and similar groups: Jews in these groups who have converted to Christianity but continue to observe various Jewish practices are no longer considered part of the Jewish community in the usual sense. They do, however, deserve respect and the right to practice their religion freely.

Common Misunderstandings and Stereotypes

"The Jews are the 'Chosen People' who consider themselves better than others."
The Jews' status as chosen people signifies not superiority but special obligations. Jews view themselves as having a mission to live a monotheistic and ethical lifestyle, but do not view themselves as morally or socially superior to any other religious or ethnic group.

"Jews are 'Christ-Killers.' "
Though some Jewish leaders at the time of Jesus opposed him, the leader of the Roman occupation in Judea, Pontius Pilate, had him crucified (the Roman form of capital punishment) for fear he would start a revolution against Roman rule.

"Jews rejected 'their Messiah.' "
Jews do not accept Jesus of Nazareth as the Messiah because (1) his followers claimed he was a divine being (contrary to Jewish belief); and (2) they do not see that his coming ushered in the expected period of peace and justice, and an end to the persecution of Jews.

"Hanukkah is the 'Jewish Christmas.' "
Hanukkah's origins are completely distinct from those of Christmas. Jews do not celebrate Christmas because they do not accept Jesus as Messiah.

"Jews are greedy, as typified in the expression, 'Jew them down.' "
During the Middle Ages in Europe, Jews were forced into the profession of money lending because Christians considered it forbidden by the Bible. Because Jews were not allowed to own land or participate in most trades until modern times in Europe, they tended to work as small shop keepers and pawn brokers. Jewish

association with these professions led to the stereotype of Jews as greedy or obsessed with money. Shakespeare's play *The Merchant of Venice*—about Shylock, a wealthy and stingy Jew—both reflected and perpetuated this image.

Classroom Concerns

The period surrounding the Christian holidays of Christmas and Easter can be difficult for Jewish children in public schools. It is recommended that classroom activities should not include Christmas or Easter pageants or make it appear that everyone observes these holidays. School activities scheduled on Friday evenings are also a problem because of the Jewish Sabbath.

It is recommended that the Nazi genocide against the Jewish people, the Holocaust, be discussed in the upper grades. It is both a unique event in history and an example of the "crimes against humanity" that have been so numerous in modern times and which humankind must strive never to repeat.

Population Data

There are about 14 million Jews worldwide, with the largest concentrations in the United States (5.5 million) and Israel (5 million).[2]

—B.H.

Notes

1.   The percentages of Jews in each branch are taken from a 1990 survey by the Council of Jewish Federations under the direction of Barry A. Kosmin. A total of 2,441 randomly selected Jewish individuals were interviewed. The percentages of Jews in each branch do not tally 100 percent because some respondents to the survey described themselves as "just Jewish" (5 percent) or "something else/don't know" (5 percent).

2.   Robert Famighetti, ed. *World Almanac and Book of Facts* (New York: World Almanac Books/Funk & Wagnalls, 1997), 646.

Further Reading

Fackenheim, Emil L. *What Is Judaism? An Interpretation for the Present Age*. New York: Summit Books, 1987.

Greenstein, Howard R. *Judaism—An Eternal Covenant*. Philadelphia: Fortress Press, 1983.

Neusner, Jacob. *The Way of Torah: An Introduction to Judaism*. 5th ed. Belmont, CA: Wadsworth, 1993.

Seltzer, Robert M. *Jewish People, Jewish Thought: The Jewish Experience in History*. New York: Macmillan, 1980.

Dream Catchers trap bad dreams that come in the night in the web, where they remain until the morning when they are dispersed by the sun's rays or the evaporation of the dew. Only the good dreams know their way through the hole in the center of the web and to the sleeping person.

Native American Religions

Origins

Hunting people crossed the dry Bering Straits to North America more than 20,000 years ago. By the time of Columbus (who mistakenly called them "Indians," thinking he had arrived in India), there were more than 300 cultural groups, each speaking its own language and practicing its own religion.

Beliefs

Everything in nature is alive, dynamic, real, and significant; and there is nothing beyond nature. American Indians pay careful attention to nature and show respect toward it. Nature changes—day to night, youth to old age, seed to plant. Nature also transforms—from human to animal to divine, material to immaterial, ignorance to wisdom. As one among other beings of nature, humans participate in this change, thereby contributing to the world's stability and continuity. Shamans [SHAW-muns], medicine men and women, acquire sacred helpers who cure illness, locate game, and retrieve lost souls. Priests don masks and dance as gods in rituals that bring about good things and enable changes to occur. Nature is inhabited by divine beings to whom Native Americans offer prayers or sacrifice. Other sorts of beings, both helpful and dangerous, dwell in the forests, lakes, streams, oceans, air, and under the ground. The aims of religious practice are to keep on good terms with all the beings of nature, maintain personal and communal health, and live a long and successful life.

Sacred Books/Scriptures

Indians had no writing. They remembered their sacred histories, or myths, through singing, dancing, storytelling, carving, drawing, and ritual. Myths explain how everything came to be the way it is. They teach Native Americans how to live and what will happen to them after this life. By enacting the myths in rituals, ceremonies, and art, Native Americans actualize the events of the myths in their own lives.

Practices

All tribes have one or more religious leaders, often including a shaman. Some Native Americans use amulets, charms, and songs to contact the sacred world. Others rely on visions to acquire a guardian spirit. In addition to creation myths, most Native American religions have stories of other sacred beings. One of the most common and widespread stories is about a shape-changing "trickster" who upsets the normal order of things but also brings about positive changes. All Native American religions incorporate dancing, singing, and drumming or rattling into their ceremonies.

Two widespread practices are the Sacred Pipe and the Sweat Lodge. Tobacco is used to communicate with sacred beings and to heal. The pipe symbolizes the cosmos, creation, and the proper relationship between humans and sacred beings. Each participant, sitting in a circle, smokes the pipe and extends it in six directions (north, south, east, west, up, down). The Sweat Lodge is also symbolic—its domed shape represents the world. Participants pour water on heated stones and are purified spiritually and physically by the steam.

Characteristic practices in each of the major cultural areas include:

Arctic. The Inuit [IN-you-it] Eskimo perform hunting rituals involving taboos (especially regarding menstruating women), amulets, songs, and drums. Shamans, using drums, enter trances to locate game or recover lost souls.

Far North. Algonquin [al-GONE-kwin] people tell stories about a cultural hero who, often by mistake, changes the landscape into the way it now appears. Shamans enter a tent and call upon the spirits, who shake the tent violently upon their arrival.

Great Basin. The Washo [WAH-she] hold an annual Big Time ceremony celebrating the harvest of wild crops and includes gambling, trading, dancing, and feasting. A girl's puberty is celebrated in a public ritual that initiates her into womanhood.

Plateau. Boys and girls of the Flathead tribe obtain guardian spirits through visions. The guardian is "forgotten" until adulthood, when it is then remembered and becomes a soul partner whose loss imperils the owner's life. A Spirit Dance is an occasion for singing about guardian spirits, dancing, and initiating youths into adulthood.

California. *Southern*: At puberty, Luiseño [lu-ee-SEN-yoh] girls are "cooked" in heated pits to initiate them into womanhood. Jimsonweed is used to obtain a vision in a youth's initiation ceremony, and an annual mourning ceremony includes the burning of effigies of the dead, new clothes, or other property. *Central*: Maido [MY-do] masked dancers impersonate the creator-hero in a ceremony that indoctrinates youths into tribal ways. *Northwestern*: Hupa [HOO-paw] dancers display possessions of wealth such as white deerskins, strings of dentalium shells, and large obsidian knives in a dance of world renewal.

Northwest. The Potlatch is an occasion for Kwakiutl [KWA-kee-you-tl] families to give away large amounts of wealth in exchange for certain rights, ranks, and privileges. Family status is represented in totem poles, which are like coats of arms. In one initiation ritual, a boy is taken away by a cannibal monster and readmitted to society through an elaborate drama in which his savage nature is tamed.

Southwest. The Apache [uh-PATCH-ee] celebrate a girl's puberty in a public ceremony in which she becomes White Painted Woman, bringing blessings to the tribe. In the *kachina* [kuh-CHEE-nuh] dances of the Hopi [HOPE-ee], *kachinas* (spirits of the dead) bring rain, happiness, and health. The Navaho [NAH-vuh-ho], in their "chantways," use sand paintings for curing and maintaining the order, or beauty, of nature.

Southeast. For Cherokee [CHAIR-o-kee] people, bathing in running water is a daily ritual. Men acquire war honors through brave deeds, receive new names, and often record their honors by tattooing their bodies. In the Green Corn ceremony, people celebrate the harvest of corn, resolve conflicts of the past year, are purified and revitalized, and join in the renewal of the new year.

Northeast. A sick person is cured by initiation into a secret society. The initiation involves "shooting" the patient with a sacred shell and then extracting the shell along with the illness. Men in the False Face Society of the Iroquois wear oddly distorted masks and sweep away disease by high-spirited pranks and dances. In the Big House ceremony of the Delaware, the order of the world is re-created in the design of the ceremonial Big House itself, and the order of time is renewed through the new year's ritual of the Good White Path.

Plains. Although acquiring a guardian through visions or dreams is widespread, the ritual of the "vision quest" is most at home here. Lakota [luh-KOH-tuh] men elect to undergo an ordeal of isolation for several days, without food or drink. Power and healing often accompany the vision. The Sun Dance is celebrated in a specially built sacred lodge. Men dance around the central pole of the lodge, often attached to it by lines tied to skewers of wood pierced through the skin of their chests. The pole is a tree that represents the cosmos. By pledging to undertake the dance, men undergo a ritual rebirth that renews not only their lives, but the life of the tribe as well.

All Cultural Areas. Two institutions arising from contact with Europeans are the Ghost Dance, a round dance believed to drive away all non–Native Americans, return the dead to life, and renew the world; and the Native American Church, in which peyote, a hallucinogenic cactus (eaten to induce "visions"), is used as a sacrament in an all-night spiritual ceremony.

Main Subgroups

Although each tribe has its own religion, some religious practices—such as the Ghost Dance and the Native American Church—cross tribal borders. Native Americans historically were hunters and gatherers, farmers, or both. Because of restrictions imposed by the reservation system, few Native Americans have opportunities to follow a hunting life, but some of the ceremonies and beliefs of hunters, such as the Vision Quest, are still practiced. Some Native Americans—e.g., the Navajo—are pastoralists; others—Hopi and Cherokee—are farmers; and still others—Kwakiutl—are seafaring fishers. Unfortunately, all too many Native Americans live in poverty or near-poverty, with limited opportunities for employment. As discussed in "Practices" above, tribes have been classified and divided into the following cultural areas: Arctic, Far North, Great Basin, Plateau, California, Northwest, Southwest, Southeast, Northeast, and Plains.

Common Misunderstandings and Stereotypes

With so many tribes, it is impossible to generalize. Nearly anything one can say about Native Americans can become a stereotype. Columbus's misnomer "Indian" is deeply ingrained in American culture. They have been called savages, demons, or innocent and gentle nobles; and classified as primitive, illiterate, and uncivilized. A Native American male has been called *brave*, *buck*, and *redskin*, and a Native American woman has been called *squaw*. Clichés include: "going on the warpath," "burying the hatchet," "going to the happy hunting ground," "Indian giver," and "speaking with a forked tongue." Stereotyped Native Americans go to powwows, drink firewater, carry papooses, and live in teepees or wigwams. They believe in the Great Spirit, say "How," carry tomahawks, stand stoically in the way of progress, and are disappearing: "The only good Indian is a dead Indian!"

The list goes on, but Native Americans are not disappearing, and their religions are as complex and sophisticated as many of the more familiar world religions.

They present a challenge to the teacher, for they represent a religious way of life that contrasts sharply with the dominant value orientations of the United States. They are the first people of this land, the foundation of our history. Thus, their religious values must be taken into account in painting a more complete, honest picture of the history and experience of all Americans.

"White Man's Indian," the image of what Native Americans *should* be, often prevents others from seeing Native Americans as they truly are. Many speak English rather than their tribal language, live in cities such as Los Angeles and Phoenix, are married to non–Native Americans (or are themselves children of such marriages), and are active members of Christian churches or other religious organizations. At the same time, they work for tribal self-determination and are proud of their Native American heritage. Change is a central experience in tribal religions. In various degrees, Native Americans continue to change to meet the challenges of living in the modern United States, but nevertheless remain Native American.

Classroom Concerns

It is recommended that teachers should avoid imitating Native American dance, dress, and singing. Dressing in buckskins, whooping with hand to mouth, and dancing by stomping on the ground only serve to perpetuate stereotypes that insult Native Americans. When attending religious ceremonies, do not take pictures, make sketches, or take notes; and dress in accordance with the sacredness of the occasion. Celebrations are not all solemn; many involve clowning, merry-making, and even obscenity. All ceremonies are, however, sacred.

It is not possible to teach about Native Americans in general. Tell the sacred stories of those who live (or lived) on the same land that you live on now. Teach the meanings of Native American city, state, and geographic names—for example, Seattle (chief of the Dwamish), Chicago ("place of the wild onion"), and Mississippi ("big river")—and tell the stories related to the naming of these places. Teach the history of Native American religions through the stories of the native peoples who are closest at hand, and let these stories suggest other stories, from all over the United States, that are waiting to be told. For example, if you live in Maine, you could tell about how Gluscap made the Penobscot River when he cut down a yellow birch. Be sure to teach the entire history, including what has happened to native peoples since the Europeans arrived.

Population Data

Population estimates at the time of Columbus ranged from less than 1 million to more than 10 million. The Native American population in the United States is currently about 2 million, with about half living on reservations. Significant population reduction can be attributed to genocide and its aftermath. By the mid-1800s, the Native American population may have been no more than a quarter of a million people. This decline in numbers since the time of Columbus was caused by warfare, malnutrition, disease, and massacre. Native Americans were caught up in the wars of the English, French, and Spanish. They were denied their land base for farming and hunting; they were not resistant to diseases—especially smallpox and tuberculosis—introduced by Europeans; and they were slaughtered outright when they got in the way of progress. Los Angeles has the largest city population of Native Americans, and Oklahoma the largest state population.

—J.H.

Further Reading

Gill, Sam. *Native American Religions: An Introduction*. Belmont, CA: Wadsworth, 1982.

———. *Native American Traditions: Sources and Interpretations*. Belmont, CA: Wadsworth, 1983.

Hultkrantz, Ake. *Native Religions of North America: The Power of Visions and Fertility*. San Francisco: Harper & Row, 1987.

Sullivan, Lawrence E., ed. *Native American Religions: North America*. New York: Macmillan, 1989.

New Age Religion

Origins

By definition, the New Age refers to a number of loosely knit interests, orientations, practices, and beliefs. These have their origins primarily in non-mainstream and nonscientific or pseudo-scientific pursuits, including the mystical and magical. The New Age does not refer to any single and central organization, belief, creed or dogma, community, or scripture that would in any way unify this mind-set. From one standpoint, it is based on a rejection at most, a down-play at least, or perhaps even an unorthodox application of that type of knowledge recognized by the scientific method. Science and scientific knowledge can be placed on a lower rung of knowledge by some New Age practitioners, or the New Age can enthusiastically adapt scientific inquiry to investigate phenomena outside the scope of ordinary scientific research.

In short, the New Age advocates two seemingly contradictory pursuits: (1) It revisits those practices, philosophies, and beliefs that were dominant in pre-Enlightenment[1] times. To a large degree, therefore, it is a reformulation and in some instances, a reinterpretation of a number of ancient practices and beliefs. (2) It applies scientific methodology to the investigation, for instance, of such practices as the paranormal.

Among the philosophies that have been incorporated from ancient times, for instance, are Neoplatonism, Gnosticism,[2] Hinduism (especially the Vedânta philosophy and practices such as *kundalinî yoga* with its attendant teachings of the *cakras*[3] [CHA-kruhs], Buddhism (especially Vajrayâna or Apocalyptic Buddhism), and Sufism (Islamic mysticism).

More recent movements or individual teachings that have contributed to the New Age movement and that may be considered direct descendants are the teachings of Emanuel Swedenborg (1688–1772); Franz Mesmer (1734–1815); freemasonry; Rosicrucianism; transcendentalism; mesmerism; spiritualism; Theosophy (more specifically, the teachings of the modern Theosophical movement[4] represented especially through the teachings of H. P. Blavatsky, Annie Besant, W. Q. Judge, and Charles W. Leadbeater, among others); New Thought; the Native American religious experience and pre-Christian nature religions (paganism); and a host of other more immediate and derivative movements, such as the Human Potential movement and transpersonal psychology. New Age, seen in this

108

light, is an outgrowth of the esoteric and metaphysical traditions that became prominent in the nineteenth century.

The contemporary roots of the New Age movement are more a matter of conjecture. Most put the date of its first appearance in the early 1970s or even the 1960s. J. Gordon Melton[5] has proposed the origins to be in "light" groups (those groups that combined Theosophical teachings and channeling), one of the most prominent of which was the spiritual community of Findhorn in northern Scotland, founded in 1962 by Peter and Eileen Caddy. It was and remains a community that emphasizes humans working in harmony with nature.

What seems more likely, however, was the intermixing and crossbreeding of Theosophically oriented groups, New Thought organizations, the Human Potential movement, and transpersonal psychology by individuals searching for the spiritual answers that were not provided by either the mainstream Western religions or by science. This led to a host of practices and variations of the philosophies from the East and from Western antiquity.

Beliefs

There are several key beliefs in New Age spirituality:

1. A tendency to accept a form of monism, meaning that at the base of the diversity of the universe, there is a fundamental unity. In the intellectual or metaphysical approach, this echoed Hindu Vedânta philosophy in its strictest sense. As an exercise and training path, it reflects Tantric Hinduism.[6] In the West the German Idealistic tradition taught that all reality is ultimately spiritual, a teaching that echoed Neoplatonism and the theology of Emanuel Swedenborg.

2. An expression of monism is pantheism, which teaches that the divine is within all that exists. The underlying assumption is that because the divine is inherently good, and because humanity is either a spark of or part of the divine, then humanity is fundamentally good. Again, variations of the basic idea reflect Swedenborg's teaching, Neoplatonism, and the cabalistic (i.e., Jewish mystical) speculation of the unfolding of the creative power of God.

3. A tendency by many to accept the reality of rebirth or reincarnation, a worldwide belief that most advocates connect with *karma*.

4. The wide acceptance of the Hindu teaching of *karma*: Good actions lead to good consequences, and bad actions to bad consequences. Should consequences not be borne out in the present life, they will in a future life.

5. Presence of the role of transformation, a religious experience that is not much different from the "born again" experience of evangelical Christians or the "peak experience" of psychologist Abraham Maslow. Such a transformation is not limited to individuals but also applies to society and indeed to the whole of humanity.

6. Presence of the corollary to transformation—the role of healing, for physical and mental healing is a sign of spiritual healing or transformation.

7. A spirit of optimism: Transformation is indeed within the reach of all people, and they can achieve the ultimate goal with the right technique.

8. An emphasis on the "New," that a New World Order will come about. This was originally popularized as the "Age of Aquarius," an expression popular in the 1960s but employed extensively in the nineteenth and earlier twentieth centuries in astrological (and Theosophical) circles. It referred to the time when the Sun will be in the constellation or zodiacal sign Aquarius at the spring equinox rather than the constellation Pisces (Piscean Age). If the present Piscean Age is characterized as an age of disillusionment, the new Aquarian Age will bring, eventually, an age of peace, prosperity, and the end of discrimination—but only after a time of cataclysm and war, according to many forecasters. Similarly, the Harmonic Convergence of August 16 and 17, 1987, celebrated the next step in humanity's spiritual evolution. It is around this time (the late 1980s), coincidentally, that the expression "New Age" began to take hold in the popular imagination.

9. Psychic powers are very likely to be accepted.

10. A tendency to place more reliance on symbolic, as opposed to a literal, interpretation of myths, art, and objects of nature, which in turn may have multiple layers of meaning. Symbolic meaning as a key to understanding the cosmos was a popular form of interpretation in the Middle Ages and the Renaissance, mainly due to such individuals as Saint Basil and Saint Ambrose, the Neoplatonism of Plotinus, and such works as the *Book of Dreams* of Artemidorus (third century C.E. philosopher), and the *Hieroglyphica* (book of Egyptian hieroglyphic signs) of Horapollo[7] (fifth century C.E. philosopher).

Sacred Books/Scriptures

There is no common scripture for New Age practitioners. Instead, they draw upon the writings of many religious traditions and philosophers (see "Beliefs" above).

Practices

The New Age includes practices based on several assumptions. First, the practices range from a maintenance of or a return to physical, mental, and spiritual health for the transformation of the individual and society. Second, many (but not all) of the practices are occult in nature, occult referring to secret knowledge, that is, knowledge closed to public access and possessed only by small numbers of groups and individuals who are generally initiated into this knowledge (gnostic or liberating knowledge). Generally, this knowledge covers forces, powers, or laws that exist in the world but cannot be discovered by sensual or empirical observation. Such forces can be manipulated by certain physical, verbal, or mental practices that have come under the rubric of New Age practice.

Some of the practices are ancient, many of which are based on forms of psychic reading or divination (foretelling the future):

Akâshic records. These records may be considered Cosmic Memory, referring to the storing of every thought, emotion, and event in the *âkâsha* or astral light (literally, the "ether") which can in turn be read, heard, or seen by those sensitive to these records. The Akashic Records appears in the writings and pronouncements of the America occult diagnostician of disease, Edgar Cayce (1871–1945).

Astrology. Divination based on the position of the planets and stars.

Aura reading. Divination based on the energy that is emitted from all things in nature, visible only through clairvoyance and Kirlian photography.

Channeling. The same as mediumship in spiritualism, in which a spirit, usually of a deceased individual who has lived hundreds or even thousands of years ago, communicates through the channeler, who is usually in a trance, giving advice or teaching.

I Ching. The ancient Chinese classic *I Ching* (*Book of Changes*)—divination based on the interpretation of 64 broken and solid lines arranged in hexagrams that appear in the text.

Numerology. Divination based on the notion that all things are expressed in numbers and the cosmos is a mathematical construct.

Palmistry. Divination based on reading the lines and mounds of palms and fingers.

Pendulum movements. Divination based on dowsing, in which the pendulum is supposedly sensitive to energy emitted from objects and living beings, and this energy can be communicated by its swinging movements.

Psychometry. Divination based on handling objects associated with persons or events.

Retrocognition. Divination about a past event through psychic power; or precognition—divination about a future event.

Runes. Ancient Teutonic writing that indicated for those who were able to decipher the symbols that they possessed magical powers.

Scrying. Divination based on clairvoyant visions arising from gazing on an object such as a crystal ball or mirror.

Tarot cards. Divination based on a set of playing cards showing emblemic figures that, when played in a certain way, foretell the future for the individual. The Tarot cards also have a deeper meaning which associates them with the Tree of Life of the Cabala (Kabbala): the Cabala originally referred to Jewish mystical thought and later, during the Renaissance, to Christian Cabala. The Tree of Life reveals the relation between God, humans, and the cosmos.

New Age also emphasizes the maintenance or improvement of the body's health through a number of practices that are by no means exclusive to this religion. Such practices include:

Acupuncture. The insertion of needles into the skin at certain points of the body that help to unblock the flow of the vital force, or *ch'i*, that circulates through the body.

Acupressure. The application of pressure using the hands and fingers on those spots where needles are ordinarily inserted in acupuncture.

Reflexology. The application of pressure from the fingers and thumb on those spots on the ball and sole of the foot that are believed to be connected to other parts and organs of the body.

Shiatsu. Japanese massage and acupressure.

Therapeutic touch. Healing by holding the hands over that area of the body that is in need of healing, or manipulating the body's energy field with hand strokes.

In general, any practice that is considered part of holistic medicine is accepted by the New Age, including alternative interpretations of the body's map. These include the acceptance of the Hindu and Buddhist yogic *cakras* (psychic centers) and the *kundalinî* (psycho-divine potency) that passes through them. Various meditative techniques may also be included as well.

Crystals (the general term for any gem or stone that possesses a molecular pattern reflected on its surface) have become popular since the 1980s for physical and mental healing, the alleviation of stress, and the arousal of higher consciousness and creativity.

Another characteristic of New Age is its music. The general nature of New Age music is to induce relaxation and to serve as an aid in healing.

Main Subgroups

Strictly speaking, there are no subgroups because there is no mainline New Age Church. It is better to regard New Age religion in the manner considered above under Origins. The New Age, therefore, refers more to a network rather than a movement, which in turn adopts and adapts ideas and practices from the previous age and redirects and incorporates them in what is interpreted to be the New Age. Furthermore, with regard to those who participate in the New Age ideas and practices, Grace Davie has argued two attitudes: "believing without belonging" and "belonging without believing."[8] Participation does not include a service or worship, but rather being in the milieu of the audience, i.e., a group that is not bonded as a cohesive unit.

If the New Age portends a New World Order, so to speak, a legitimate question might arise regarding its relationship to a movement that closely resembles it from the preceding age, New Thought.

There are similarities and differences between New Thought and New Age movements. The very names of these broad-based movements can easily cause confusion, especially when they share so much in common. Among their similarities are:

1. Ideas that derive from many of the same sources, including Neoplatonism, which teaches that the soul is the divine spark of God; Hindu Vedânta monistic philosophy; the Swedenborgian view that spiritual laws are both correspondent to and the cause of natural laws; the mesmeric view of a magnetic fluid (much like the Hindu *prâna* and the Chinese *ch'i*) that permeates the universe connecting all things and humans, and Mesmer's experiments with hypnotism; and the transcendentalism of Ralph Waldo Emerson (1803–1882), who wrote that "Mind is the only reality of which men and all natures are better or worse reflectors."

2. A sense of optimism.

3. An emphasis on the one power in the universe, which is seen as good.

4. An emphasis on alternative medicine.

These ideas are reflected in the Declaration of Principles followed by the churches affiliated in the International New Thought Alliance. These would very likely be accepted, in whole or in part, by a majority of New Agers, whether or not they have affiliations with New Thought churches:

1. The Oneness of God and Humans;

2. Freedom in matters of belief;

3. The Good is supreme, eternal, universal;

4. The Kingdom of God is within us;

5. "We" can heal the sick through prayer;

6. Belief in God as the Universal Wisdom, Love, Life, Truth, Power, Peace, Plenty, Beauty, Joy;

7. The idea that a human's mental states are carried forward into manifestation and become his or her experience through the Creative Law of Cause and Effect;

8. Divine Nature expresses itself through humanity and is manifested as health, wisdom, love, life, truth;

9. A human being is an invisible spiritual dweller within a human body;

New Age and New Thought, one might argue, are more similar than different. Yet, there are differences. New Thought is older, originating in the 1880s and

1890s, about 100 years prior to New Age. It is a descendent of the teachings of Phineas P. Quimby (1802–1866), who emphasized "mental healing," which is based on the idea that disease was caused by delusion and error fixed within the mind. This doctrine, called by Quimby the Science of Health, attracted a number of followers, among whom were Mary Baker Eddy, the founder of the Church of Christian Science (see the chapter "Christian Science").

It was Emma Curtis Hopkins, however, who contributed more to the dissemination of New Thought ideas and institutions by training a number of students in her Christian Science Theological Seminary in Chicago. These students would later found separate organizations: Myrtle and Charles Fillmore, founders of the Unity School of Christianity; Annie Rix Militz, founder of the Homes of Truth; Melinda Cramer, founder of Divine Science; and Ernest Holmes, founder of the Church of Religious Science in 1926. Hopkins was important in helping to differentiate New Thought from Christian Science, first by breaking from Mary Baker Eddy and her church, and second by training a core of ministers (about 100, mostly women) to teach and practice their own variations of Christian Science, which by the end of the nineteenth century became known as New Thought. Out of this came the New Thought Alliance, later called the International New Thought Alliance, which comprises a number of independent church organizations.

A second major difference between New Thought and New Age represents more of a psychological attitude toward human conditions. New Thought was never reactionary or revolutionary in its view of the world. The teaching of Mind was the one way to deal with the problems of the individual, society, and world because they were all subject to Mind, which is inherently good.

New Age, however, perceived the situation in less optimistic terms. There was a sense that many practices and beliefs were beyond the individual's control, resulting in more pessimism with the present age. Only the replacement of the Dark Age or preceding age with a New Age—what originally was called the Aquarian Age—would change things for the better. To do so, new practices and new ideas not related to the dominant mold of the Old Age were adopted as means of making people whole. These included the occult practices (see "Practices") that normally would not be accepted in New Thought but certainly accepted in the New Age.

A third difference centers on who is susceptible to healing. New Thought restricts it to individuals, but New Age extends it to the entire planet.

Common Misunderstandings and Stereotypes

"The New Age movement is composed of a bunch of weirdos."

New Age practitioners are clearly out of the mainstream of American religion, but their ideas have a consistency and logic that is neither weird nor wicked. They seek the betterment of their followers and of humankind generally through the means described above. Moreover, many traditional Christian, Jewish, and other religious people have adopted one or more of the practices of New Age—especially those relating to health—without accepting the system as a whole.

Population Data

No estimate can be given since it is next to impossible to determine who is and who is not a full-time, committed member of the New Age network.

—*J.S.*

Notes

1. The Enlightenment refers to a movement in Western philosophy in the seventeenth and eighteenth centuries that was skeptical of Christian beliefs and accepted only those biblical and theological teachings that could be reconciled with reason and the methods of science.

2. Gnosticism is a religious philosophy that originated in the Near East at about the same time as Christianity. It stresses *gnosis* (esoteric or mystical knowledge) as the key to salvation.

3. *Cakras* are energy centers in the spiritual body of a person, each of which is associated with a Hindu deity.

4. Theosophy is a movement combining Western interest in the occult and mystical with Eastern religious philosophy. It strives for the unity of humankind, the study of comparative religion and philosophy, and the uncovering of the powers latent in humankind.

5. James R. Lewis and J. Gordon Melton, eds., "New Thought and the New Age," in *Perspectives on the New Age* (Albany: SUNY Press, 1992), 20.

6. The term Tantra refers to a body of texts. As a general term, it refers to those practices and movements (sects or lineages) that emphasize the worship of the Female energy (*shakti*) and for adepts to gain this power in conjunction with the Unchanging Masculine Being. In cosmic terms, it is the Female energy that permeates the universe. Different techniques are employed, one of which involved *kundalinî yoga*: the technique of raising the latent power *kundalinî* resting at the base of the spine upward through the power centers known as *cakras*. In Tantrism, there is the fundamental assumption of an identity between absolute and phenomenal existence. In New Age metaphysics, the notions of bioenergetics, biodynamics, and synergy reflect the world in terms of energy and vibration.

7. The *Hieroglyphica* probably had the greatest influence on scholars of the Renaissance era regarding Egyptian symbols. See the *Hieroglyphics of Horapollo*, translated by George Boas with a new foreword by Anthony Grafton (Princeton, NJ: Princeton University Press, 1993 [originally copyrighted in 1950 and renewed in 1979]). On the *Book of Dreams (Oreirocriticon)*, see Claes Blum, *Studies in the Dream-Book of Artemidorus* (Uppsala, Sweden: Almqvist & Wiksell, 1936).

8. "Believing Without Belonging: Is This the Future of Religion in Britain?" *Social Compass* 37 (1990): 4, quoted in *Che cos'è il New Age* by Jean Vernette. Translated form the French by Stefano Viviani (Carnago [Varese], Italy: Sugarco Edizioni S.r.l., 1992), 12. This appears in Massimo Introvigne's introduction to the book.

Secular Humanism/ Atheism

Origins

Secular Humanism, which considers humanity as a substitute for God, is partly rooted in the Enlightenment movement of the eighteenth century within Western philosophy. The Enlightenment philosophers, while not denying God's existence, were critical of the nonrational elements of religion such as belief in miracles. One offshoot of the Enlightenment was deism, the notion that God created the world but then left it up to humanity to work out its destiny with no divine intervention. Deism profoundly influenced the founding fathers of the United States, including Benjamin Franklin, George Washington, Thomas Jefferson, James Madison, and John Adams. This is particularly true of the framing of the First Amendment's provisions for no official, state-sponsored church and for the free exercise of any religion by United States citizens.

Along with the Enlightenment, the other principal sources of Humanism were the ideas of French philosopher August Comte (1798–1857), who organized a Church of Humanity in Paris; and the American Humanistic Association (AHA), begun in the 1920s. In 1933 the AHA, which included prominent American philosopher John Dewey, issued a Humanist Manifesto, which rejected supernatural explanations for the origins of the universe and regarded humanity as part of nature. Several Unitarian ministers were also prominent in the movement (see the chapter "Unitarian Universalism"). In 1973 the AHA issued a second manifesto stressing the importance of technology in preserving the environment, alleviating poverty, reducing disease, prolonging life, and discovering new ways of making human existence more meaningful.

Beliefs

Secular Humanists reject belief in a supernatural being or beings and are, in effect, atheists. They believe in humanity and its ability to solve human problems without divine assistance. Philosophical or so-called existential atheists, such as French philosopher Jean-Paul Sartre, argue that to be authentically free in the universe, it is necessary that God(s) not exist, for their existence would limit human freedom.

Sacred Books/Scriptures

There is no single writing that Secular Humanists accept as normative for their movement. Documents such as Humanist Manifestos I and II are certainly important, but so are the writings of August Comte, British philosopher Bertrand Russell, and many others.

Practices

In place of clergy, the AHA licenses counselors to conduct weddings and funerals for Humanists. Not surprisingly, there are no rituals within the Humanist movement. However, some self-described Humanists belong to the Unitarian Universalist Association and participate in the non-theistic services of this group (see the chapter "Unitarian Universalism"). There are also small Humanist groups such as the Ethical Culture Society and the Society for Humanistic Judaism, whose tenets are similar to those of the AHA and Unitarian Universalists. The Society for Humanistic Judaism does conduct services, but they are non-theistic.

Main Subgroups

It is important to realize that many Secular Humanists/atheists are not affiliated with any official group but simply hold a philosophical position that parallels that of "card-carrying" humanists. There are several Humanistic organizations in the United States, such as the AHA and Ethical Culture Society; the Council for Democratic and Secular Humanism, which publishes a magazine *Free Inquiry*; and the Alliance of Secular Humanist Societies, with local affiliates around the country. Finally, there is a global alliance of Humanists, the International Humanist Ethical Union.

Common Misunderstandings and Stereotypes

"Secular Humanists hate religion and seek to suppress it."
Although Humanists do not accept the religious teachings of Christianity or any other faith, they respect religious people insofar as they work for the betterment of humanity. Humanists in no way seek to keep religious people from practicing their faiths.

"Secular Humanists are godless and immoral."

The term *secular* is sometimes used by conservative religionists to cast Humanists in a bad light. Though Humanists reject belief in God(s), it does not follow that they lack morals. In fact, they tend to be very ethical individuals with a deep dedication to improving living conditions for people everywhere.

Classrooms Concerns

Teachers should try to be sensitive to the unique situation of a child whose parents are Humanists or atheists. Teachers will very often be unaware of the nonreligious background of such children. It is important for teachers not to criticize Humanism/atheism, even though it might not agree with their world view.

Humanist students may be reluctant to salute the flag because of the words "under God" in the Pledge of Allegiance. They should be informed that they may either stand silently while other students do so or be excused from class during the recitation.

Population Data

The *World Almanac and Book of Facts*[1] cites that there are 220 million atheists worldwide (1.6 million in North America, with more than 1 million in the United States alone). A study by Kosmin and Lachman[2] found that 8.2 percent of the adult population in the United States describe themselves as having no religious affiliation. How many of these would actually describe themselves as Secular Humanists or atheists is unclear. However, if we assume that the majority of the children of the nonreligious are also unaffiliated, we have perhaps as many as 20 million Americans in the nonreligious category.

—B.H.

Notes

1.   Robert Famighetti, ed. *World Almanac and Book of Facts* (New York: World Almanac Books/Funk & Wagnalls, 1997), 646.

2.   Barry A. Kosmin and Seymour P. Lachman, *One Nation Under God: Religion in Contemporary American Society* (New York: Harmony Books, 1993), 3.

Further Reading

Kurtz, Paul. *The Humanist Alternative: Some Definitions of Humanism*. Buffalo, NY: Prometheus Press, 1973.

Martin, David A. *A General Theory of Secularization*. San Francisco: Harper & Row, 1979.

Phifer, Kenneth W. *The Faith of a Humanist*. Boston: Unitarian Universalist Association (undated).

This Sikh symbol, known as the khanda, consists of a double-edged sword (khanda: representing the cutting of Truth from Falsehood) surrounded by a circle (chakar) symbolizing eternity. On either side are curved swords (kirpân), which symbolize one's spiritual aspirations and obligations to society.

Sikhism

Origins

The founder of the Sikh [seek] religion was Guru Nânak (1469–1539). Raised Hindu in the Panjab region of northern India, his religious background reflects the devotional (bhakti) traditions within Hinduism, most especially the Sant (Saint) tradition. The designation Sant applies to those poet-saints in the Panjab belonging to a loose collection of devotional groups who taught that the Supreme God was beyond all comprehension. According to biographical accounts, Nânak opposed both Muslim fanaticism and Hindu ritual and caste by teaching his followers to meditate on God's name. As a religious teacher or spiritual guide who came face to face with God to receive his mandate, he became a Guru: one who is a spiritual guide or, according to the popular etymology, the Light (i.e., the Divine Light) that dispels darkness. To Sikhs, Guru Nânak—and all Sikh leaders who were given the title Guru—was the vehicle through which God transmitted his teaching. The Guru is therefore primarily a teacher; he is neither God nor a messiah. A follower of the Guru is known as a Sikh (disciple), hence the religion's name. By definition, a Sikh may be defined as one who is a disciple of the 10 human Gurus, from Guru Nânak to Guru Gobind (Guruship: 1675–1708, b. 1666–1708) and the sacred book that replaced the human Guru, the Guru Granth Sahib [GOO-roo grunth sa-HEEB] or Adi [AH-dee] Granth.

Beliefs

The fundamental belief is found in the opening lines of the sacred book of the Sikhs, the Guru Granth Sahib. These lines declare that God is One, Absolute, Creator, Without Fear or Hatred, Timeless, Unborn, Self-Existent, Omnipresent, and the Supreme Truth. Hindu traditional beliefs were accepted by Nânak, such as *karma* (actions and their consequences; according to Sikhs, the rewards and punishments for actions are determined by God) and the cycle of existence or rebirth. The purpose of human life is to dispel ignorance, egoism, and suffering and to achieve purity and illumination of mind by God's Grace and by constant repetition of the name of God. This practice produces a God-Conscious and Godlike person. In other words, a human cannot become God but, according to Guru Arjan (Guruship: 1581–1606, b. 1563–1606), there is ultimately no difference between God and a God-Conscious soul.

Sacred Books/Scriptures

The Guru Granth Sahib/Adi Granth is considered the living Guru of the Sikhs. This status was conferred upon it with the death of the tenth and last human Guru, Gobind, who declared shortly before his death that the Guru Granth Sahib itself be his successor. Although the Guru Granth Sahib underwent development from the time of Guru Nânak, it received its distinctive form under the fifth Guru, Arjan. It was later expanded by the last Guru, Gobind, who added hymns of his father, the ninth Guru, Tegh Bahadur Ji (Guruship 1664–1675, b. 1621–1675). The Guru Granth Sahib now consists of a standardized 1,430 pages, written in Gurmukhi script. What is unique is that Hindu and Muslim poet-saints are also included in the collection. The total number of hymns is 5,894, with the largest contribution by Guru Arjan (2,216). The basis of classification of the Guru Granth Sahib is the *râga,* which indicates a pattern of melodic notes. Because there are 31 *râgas* or melodic divisions, the bulk of the Guru Granth Sahib consists primarily of these melodic divisions or hymns: 31 or 33 divisions.

Practices

Practices include dress, life-cycle rituals, festivals, and worship in the temple (Gurdwara). Since the time of Guru Gobind, who founded the Khâlsâ, the Community of warrior-Sikhs or the initiated Sikh Brotherhood, on Vaisakhi (Baisakhi) Day (April 13) in 1699, initiated or baptized Sikhs began to share certain practices and dress. Initiated by means of the baptism ritual (Amrit) in which the candidate then becomes Khâlsâ (literally "pure") by following a strict regimen of abstaining from destructive practices such as the taking of intoxicants and tobacco, not committing adultery and infanticide, not eating the meat of animals killed in any religious ceremony, and wearing the Five Ks. The Five Ks are: (1) to leave the hair (kesh) uncut (over which a turban is worn), (2) to keep a comb (kanghâ) within the hair,

(3) to wear a steel dagger (kirpân), (4) to wear a steel bracelet (karâ), and (5) to wear a specific knee-length undergarment (kacch). All Sikh males take the name Singh (lion), and all women take the additional name Kaur (princess). These designations replaced the traditional name that indicated one's caste, an institution that was rejected by Sikhs.

Life-cycle rites include the name-giving (Nam Karan), baptism (pahul), marriage (Anand Karaj), and funeral rites. Sikhs participate in many festivals, but of those that are celebrated, five are universally observed:

Birthday of Guru Nânak. October/November.

Birthday of Guru Gobind. December 22.

Installation of the Guru Granth Sahib as Guru. Commemorates the date in 1604 when the sacred book was installed at the Golden Temple in Amritsar; celebrated September/October.

Vaisakhi (the New Year) (Baisakhi) is celebrated on April 13, a day that is especially important since the Khâlsâ order was founded on this day by Guru Gobind in 1699. Also during Guru Amar Das' Guruship (1552–1574, b. 1479), the first annual gathering of Sikhs was initiated at the center of pilgrimage, Goindwal.

Dîwâlî. A festival of light similar to the Hindu and Jain festivals of the same name, but marking the return of the sixth Guru, Har Gobind (Guruship: 1606–1644. b. 1595–1644), to the holy city of Amritsar after his release from prison (October/November).

All the festivals, open to men and women, include hymnal singing, lectures, consecrated food, and free food provided by the communal kitchen. One feature of the Gurpurb (or Gurupurab: a specific type of celebration reserved for the anniversaries of the birth, ascendancy to guruship, martyrdom, and death of the ten Gurus, the installation of the Guru Granth Sahib as the successor to the human Gurus, and the deaths of the sons of Guru Gobind) is the continuous reading of the Guru Granth Sahib, which takes about 48 hours. The dates of the Gurpurb follow a lunar calendar, so the days will vary from year to year.

Sikh temples serve a number of purposes. Services consist of singing passages from the Guru Granth Sahib, exposition of a passage by a granthi (one who is versed in the text), the concluding prayer, and the meal that is taken by the congregation.

A note about the Golden Temple and Sikh temples in general: By the eighteenth century, the city of Amritsar, the Sikh holy city wherein the Golden Temple is located, served as the gathering spot for Sikhs especially after the death of the last Guru. The Golden Temple was built during Guru Arjan's time, the foundation stone laid in 1588. It is in the midst of an artificial lake, Amritsar (the Pool of Nectar), in the city of the same name, and is the center of Sikh religious power. The Temple was attacked in June 1984 by the Indian army to flush out Sikh fundamentalists. Many hundreds or thousands of pilgrims lost their lives, leading to an animosity toward the Indian government that has not healed. A direct outcome of this attack was the assassination of the Indian prime minister, Mrs. Indira Gandhi.

Main Subgroups

Sikhs in the United States generally are of Indian, more specifically, Panjabi origin. Subgroups do exist based on the issues of Guru succession, ritual, and customs. For instance, Khâlsâ Sikhs of Guru Gobind (the Singhs) only accept the ten Gurus ending with Gobind; two reform movements, the Nâmdhârîs (founded by Sâîn Sâhib, d. 1862) and Nirankârîs (founded by Dyâl Dâs [1783–1855]) worship living Gurus. The first movement opposed introduction of idol worship, caste distinctions, satî (the cremation of the living wife on the funeral pyre of her deceased husband) in the Sikh community; the latter opposed the worship of idols and the adoption of Hindu marriage ritual. Nânakpanthîs are Sikhs who follow the teachings of Guru Nânak. Udâsîs, followers of Guru Nânak's son, Shri Chand, are more ascetically inclined than other groups. A twofold division may be considered to separate these and other sects: the Singhs, including the Khâlsâ or Gobind, and the Sahajdhârîs (The Easy Goers or Slow Adopters), who include the Nânakpanthîs. This by no means exhausts the number of groups that exist or have existed within the Sikh community.

One group, however, that is predominantly Western is the 3HO, or the Healthy, Happy, and Holy Organization, founded by Sardar Harbhajan Singh Puri in the 1960s. The members of this organization are recognizable by the wearing of white, Indian-style clothing and turbans by men and women. Both groups of Sikhs share in the basic beliefs and practices, with members visiting the temples of either community.

Common Misunderstandings and Stereotypes

"Why do they wear those turbans?"
The main area of concern is unfamiliarity with the dress codes of the Sikh community. Before a boy is initiated, his hair is allowed to grow with a cloth covering it. This might cause comment among other students to the discomfort of the Sikh student. If sufficiently mature, the student might be willing to explain these customs in class or in a paper.

"Should Sikh students be allowed to carry a weapon to school?"
Once initiated into practice, the Five Ks, especially leaving the hair uncut, over which a turban is worn, and carrying a steel dagger (the "dagger" is actually only a few inches long and is concealed) are clearly a concern for school officials because of the "zero tolerance" weapons policy of most schools nationwide. This is a time-honored practice among Panjabi Sikhs and so must be handled with discretion by teachers and administrators alike. Consultation with the Sikh parents is recommended. The Ninth Circuit Court of Appeals ruled in 1995 (*Cheemah v. Thompson*) that Sikh students could carry the dagger to school as long as it was sewn into its sheath.

Classroom Concerns

Sikh holidays and festivals are not generally recognized in United States schools, but it must be remembered that certain obligations have to be carried out by the Sikh community that might require the student to miss school. It is advisable that the teacher and administrator discuss with the parents ahead of time which days might require the student to be away from class.

Population Data

According to the 1991 Indian census, there are 16,259,744 Sikhs residing in India, almost 2 percent of the population. Most reside in the Panjab (12,767,697), comprising almost 63 percent of the population. Globally, according to the *World Almanac and Book of Facts*,[1] there are about 20 million Sikhs. Sikhs have emigrated to all parts of the world, including Canada, the United States, Great Britain, Africa, and other parts of Asia. The emigration was accelerated after the partition of India in 1947. The Sikhs who entered the United States and Canada were mainly professionals (doctors, teachers, and engineers), although many who came to California prior to this time worked as farm laborers. Many eventually bought farm land and now own sizable orchards and farms in California. A liberalization of the immigration laws after 1965 allowed many more Sikhs to enter. The estimated population of Sikhs in the United States is about 400,000.[1] The number of Sikh adherents to the 3HO is fairly small, about 5,000.

—J.S.

Notes

1. Robert Famighetti, ed. *World Almanac and Book of Facts* (New York: World Almanac Books/Funk & Wagnalls, 1997), 646.

Further Reading

Cole, W. Owen. *The Sikhs: Their Religious Beliefs and Practices.* London and Boston: Routledge and Kegan Paul, 1978.

Hawley, John Stratton, and Gurinder Singh Mann, eds. *Studying the Sikhs: Issues for North America.* Albany, NY: SUNY, 1993.

McLeod, W. H. *The Sikhs: History, Religion, and Society.* New York: Columbia University Press, 1989.

Unitarian Universalism

Origins

Unitarians trace their roots to such "free thinkers" of the Reformation era as Michael Servetus (1511–1553) and to liberal movements in Poland, Transylvania (part of present-day Romania), and England during the sixteenth to eighteenth centuries. Joseph Priestly, a refugee from England because of his beliefs, formed the first Unitarian church in the United States in about 1794. During the early 1800s, a number of New England Congregationalist (United Church of Christ) churches embraced Unitarianism. Universalism, begun by John Murray, was a distinct but similar movement until its merger with the Unitarians in 1961. Unitarian Universalism formed its first congregation in 1779 in Gloucester, Massachusetts.

Beliefs

Unitarian Universalists (UUs), as the name implies, reject the trinitarian nature of God and thus the divinity of Jesus. In fact, belief in God is not even required for membership. They also believe that salvation is universal, open to everyone in the world. UUs rely on their own reason and the teachings of the great religious and philosophical thinkers of all cultures for guidance. Though UUs revere the ethical teachings of Jesus, he is not their final religious authority. Hence, UUs are not considered Christian.

Sacred Books/Scriptures

There are no official scriptures; instead, UUs draw on the sacred writings of many religious traditions for inspiration and read from them and the works of poets and philosophers in their weekly services.

Practices

UUs have no sacraments as such but have rituals dedicating their children to the service of humanity, recognizing their coming of age, celebrating marriage, and remembering the dead.

UUs have Sunday services that consist of readings from various religious traditions, poets, and philosophers; a sermon; the singing of hymns; sharing of thoughts from the congregation; and a social hour afterwards.

UUs are very committed to social outreach—various activities to help people in need and to work for the passage of legislation that will better conditions for such people.

Main Subgroups

Given the tolerant and non-dogmatic characteristics of the church, there are no subgroups, though individual churches are fully independent and thus free to emphasize different styles of worship, different social service agendas, and so on.

Common Misunderstandings and Stereotypes

"Unitarian Universalists are anti-Christian."
Though UUs accept neither belief in the Trinity nor Jesus' divinity, they bear no resentment towards Christianity. In fact, they applied in the past for membership in the National Council of Churches of Christ but were denied admittance. They do, however, work cooperatively with the council and other religious groups on common concerns.

"Unitarian Universalists promote atheism."
Though UUs leave the decision about whether to believe in a higher power or God in the hands of individual members, there is no attempt whatsoever to convince people to become atheists. In fact, UUs do not actively seek converts, though they will happily explain their teachings to anyone interested.

Classroom Concerns

It is recommended that Unitarian Universalist students not be lumped under the headings of Protestant or atheist. UUs are Humanists, or non-creedal free thinkers, who may personally hold a variety of beliefs but are united by their dedication to the principles of freedom, reason, and tolerance. (See the chapter "Secular Humanism/ Atheism.")

Like other non-Christian students, UUs do not celebrate Christian holidays. Teachers should be mindful of this.

It is recommended that teachers mention to their students the number of prominent Americans who either practiced Unitarian Universalism or were sympathetic to its philosophy: Thomas Jefferson, John Adams, John Quincy Adams, Benjamin Franklin, Thomas Paine, James Madison, Ralph Waldo Emerson, Nathaniel Hawthorne, Henry Wadsworth Longfellow, Amy Lowell, Louisa May Alcott, Susan B. Anthony, and Clara Barton, among others.

Population Data

There are 141,000 Unitarian Universalists in the United States,[1] and—based on the presence of Unitarian Universalist congregations in Europe—perhaps another 10,000–20,000 worldwide.

—B.H.

Notes

1. Robert Famighetti, ed. *World Almanac and Book of Facts* (New York: World Almanac Books/Funk & Wagnalls, 1997), 645.

Further Reading

Mendelsohn, Jack. *Meet the Unitarian Universalists*. Boston: Unitarian Universalist Association, 1979.

———. *Being Liberal in an Illiberal Age: Why I Am a Unitarian-Universalist*. Boston: Beacon Press, 1985.

Annotated Bibliography

Books

Council on Islamic Education. *Teaching About Islam in the Public School Classroom: A Handbook for Educators.* 3rd ed. Fountain Valley, CA: Council on Islamic Education, 1995.
 A balanced, rich resource for teaching about Islam.

Eliade, Mircea, ed. *The Encyclopedia of Religion.* 16 vols. New York: Macmillan, 1987.
 The most detailed and comprehensive reference work in English on the world's religions; includes extensive bibliographies.

Eliade, Mircea, and Ioan Couliano. *The Eliade Guide to World Religions.* San Francisco: Harper, 1991.
 A single-volume compendium of 33 major religions. Brief entries, with annotated index and bibliographies. Useful for identifying unfamiliar religious terms.

Famighetti, Robert, ed. *World Almanac and Book of Facts.* New York: World Almanac Books/Funk & Wagnalls, 1997.

Freedman, David Noel, ed. *The Anchor Bible Dictionary.* 6 vols. New York: Doubleday, 1992.
 The most accurate and up-to-date dictionary of its kind, with articles on every aspect of biblical studies, including archaeology.

Gaddy, Barbara, T. William Hall, and Robert Marzano. *School Wars: Resolving Our Conflicts over Religion and Values.* San Francisco: Jossey-Bass, 1996.
 A balanced look at the controversies surrounding religion and education. A useful guide to help parents, teachers, and community leaders understand the background of these disputes.

Glasse, Cyril. *The Concise Encyclopedia of Islam.* New York: Harper & Row, 1989.
 Brief and informative entries on every facet of Islam.

Guastad, Edwin. *Religious History of America.* New York: Harper & Row, 1974.
 A collection of documents from the religious history of the United States, with commentary by the author. Good source of original documents.

Hatfield, John, and Benjamin Hubbard, eds. *Presence and Promise*. Long Beach: California State University Press, 1992.

Haynes, Charles, ed. *Finding Common Ground: A First Amendment Guide to Religion and Public Education*. Nashville, TN: Freedom Forum First Amendment Center at Vanderbilt University, 1994.
    The most comprehensive and useful teacher's resource manual for First Amendment issues. Includes materials for teaching about religion.

———. *Religion in American History: What to Teach and How*. Alexandria, VA: Association for Supervision and Curriculum Development, 1990.
    Nine chapters with 13 original documents, historical background, and suggestions for using the documents.

Hubbard, Benjamin, ed. *Reporting Religion: Facts and Faith*. Sonoma, CA: Polebridge Press, 1990.

———. *The Abraham Connection: A Jew, Christian and Muslim in Dialogue*. Notre Dame, IN: Crossroads Books, 1994.

Kosmin, Barry A., and Seymour P. Lachman. *One Nation Under God: Religion in Contemporary American Society*. New York: Harmony Books, 1993.

McBrien, Richard P., ed. *The HarperCollins Encyclopedia of Catholicism*. New York: HarperCollins, 1995.
    A concise, current treatment of all aspects of the Catholic tradition, with special essays on the sacraments and key figures such as Augustine and Thomas Aquinas.

McDonald, William, ed. *The New Catholic Encyclopedia*. 18 vols. New York: McGraw-Hill, 1967–79.
    A thorough treatment of all aspects of Catholicism.

Melton, J. Gordon. *Encyclopedic Handbook of Cults in America*. New York: Garland, 1992.
    Short, insightful essays on a wide range of groups that differ significantly from religious orthodoxy and cultural norms, such as Christian Science, Jehovah's Witnesses, New Age groups, Rosicrucians, Scientology, and Theosophy.

Nord, Warren. *Religion and American Education: Rethinking a National Dilemma*. Chapel Hill: University of North Carolina Press, 1995.
    A pivotal book in the dialogue on religion's place in the public school classroom. Thorough, lengthy, and controversial, but basic for educational policy making.

Roth, Cecil, and Geoffrey Widgoder, eds. *Encyclopedia Judaica*. 16 vols. Jerusalem: Keter, 1972.
    The most comprehensive reference work on Jewish religion and civilization in English. Extensive bibliographies.

Smart, Ninian. *The World's Religions.* Englewood Cliffs, NJ: Prentice-Hall, 1989.
A comprehensive treatment, with something on just about every religion that has ever existed. The classical or historical period and the modern period of each tradition is included.

Smith, Jonathan Z., and William Scott Green, eds. *The HarperCollins Dictionary of Religion.* San Francisco: Harper, 1995.
The best, most up-to-date one-volume resource on every aspect of religion worldwide.

Telushkin, Joseph. *Jewish Literacy: The Most Important Things to Know About the Jewish Religion, Its People and Its History.* New York: William Morrow, 1991.
A highly readable dictionary of all things Jewish, with brief and informative entries arranged either historically or by subject matter.

Young, William A. *The World's Religions: Worldviews and Contemporary Issues.* Englewood Cliffs, NJ: Prentice-Hall, 1995.
A clearly written survey, notable for its coverage of the ethical stances of the various religions on abortion, euthanasia, gender issues, homosexuality, war, and so on.

Periodicals

Religion and Education
A journal concerned with teaching about religions in history and culture and aimed at teaching students to participate in a pluralistic and religiously diverse world.

Religion and Public Education Network Newsletter
A publication of the Association for Supervision and Curriculum Development.

The Religion and Education Forum
A publication of the Religion and Education Special Interest Group of the American Educational Research Association.

Videotapes

Eyre, Ronald. *The Long Search.* Produced by the BBC.
This 12-part series from the mid-70s is still a remarkably vivid portrait of major religious traditions East and West.

Moyers, Bill. *The Wisdom of Faith with Huston Smith.* Public Affairs Television, 1995 (800-257-5126).
A series of dialogues between Moyers and philosopher-of-religion Smith that explores the major religions against the backdrop of religious art and architecture.

CD-ROM

Eck, Diana. *World Religions in America.*

Web Sites

The Electronically Linked Academy (TELA), Scholars Press WWW Site—
http://scholar.cc.emory.edu/

Comparative Religion—http://weber.u.washington.edu/d36/madin/

Computer-Assisted Theology on the Internet—http://info.ox.ac.uk/ctitext/theology/

Facets of Religion—http://sunfly.ub.uni-freiburg.de/religion

Ontario Centre for Religious Tolerance—http://web.canlink.com/ocrt/

Voice of the Shuttle: Religious Studies Page—http://humanitas.ucsb.edu/shuttle/
religion.html

Yahoo!–Society and Culture: Religion—http://www.yahoo.com/Society_and_
Culture/Religion/

Appendix A

Ramona Unified School District Policy Instruction

Recognition of Religious Beliefs and Customs

Preamble

Any discussion of the place of religion in public education must be grounded in the principle of religious liberty or freedom of conscience, particularly as it is embodied in this nation's First Amendment to the Constitution, which states that "Congress shall make no law respecting an establishment of religion, or prohibiting the free exercise thereof . . ." This inalienable right to religious liberty depends neither upon political authority nor upon any election but is rooted in the inviolable dignity of each person.

Statement of Purpose

The board of education endorses teaching about religion where the curriculum guides indicate it is appropriate and when the classroom atmosphere encourages both teachers and students to be responsible and to respect the rights of each person.

Such teaching must foster knowledge *about* religion, not indoctrination into religion; it should be academic, not devotional or testimonial; it should promote awareness of religion, not sponsor its practice; it should inform the students about the diversity of religious views rather than impose one particular view; and it should promote understanding of different religious views as well as respect for the rights of persons who hold such views.

Rights and Responsibility of Students/Staff

Students have the right to pray individually or in groups or to discuss their religious views with their peers so long as they are not disruptive. Because the Establishment Clause does not apply to purely private speech, students enjoy the right to read their Bibles or other scriptures, say grace before meals, pray before tests, and discuss religion with other student listeners as long as the listeners do not feel coerced or harassed. However, the right to engage in voluntary prayer does not include, for example, the right to have a captive audience listen or to compel other students to participate.

131

Teachers and school administrators, when acting in those capacities, are representatives of the state, and, in those capacities, are themselves prohibited from encouraging or soliciting student religious or anti-religious activity. Similarly, when acting in their official capacities, teachers may not engage in religious activities with their students. However, teachers may engage in private religious activity in faculty lounges.

As a general rule, students may express their religious viewpoints in the form of reports, both oral and written; homework and artwork. Teachers may not reject or correct such submissions simply because they include a religious symbol or address religious themes. Likewise, teachers may not require students to modify, include or excise religious views in their assignments, if germane. These assignments should be judged by ordinary academic standards of substance, relevance, appearance and grammar. As noted, however, teachers should not allow students to use a captive, classroom audience to proselytize or conduct religious activities.

Students have the right to distribute religious literature to their schoolmates, subject to those reasonable time, place, and manner or other constitutionally acceptable restrictions imposed on the distribution of all non-school literature. Thus, a school may confine distribution of all literature to a particular table at particular times. It may not single out religious literature for burdensome regulation.

Student participation in before- or after-school religious events on campus is permissible. School officials, acting in an official capacity, may neither discourage nor encourage participation in such an event.

Students have the right to speak to, and attempt to persuade, their peers about religious topics just as they do with regard to political topics. But school officials should intercede and stop student religious speech if it turns into religious harassment aimed at a student or a small group of students.

Student religious groups in secondary schools are permitted to meet and to have equal access to campus media to announce their meetings. Teachers may not actively participate in club activities and "non-school persons" may not control or regularly attend club meetings.

School Calendars

The school calendar should be prepared so as to minimize conflict with religious holidays of all faiths. Where conflicts are unavoidable, care should be taken to avoid tests, special projects, introduction of new concepts, and other activities that would be difficult to make up on religious holidays. Students are expected to make up missed assignments without loss of status or penalty.

Religion in Curriculum and Instruction

Students may be taught about religion, but public schools may not teach religion. As the U.S. Supreme Court has repeatedly said, "[I]t might well be said that one's education is not complete without a study of comparative religion, or the history of religion and its relationship to the advancement of civilization." It would be difficult to teach art, music, literature, and most social studies without considering religious influences.

The history of religion, comparative religion, the Bible (or other scripture) as literature (either as a separate course or within some other existing course) are all permissible public school subjects. It is both permissible and desirable to teach objectively about the role of religion in the history of the United States and other countries.

As part of the curriculum, religious literature, music, drama and the arts may be included, provided each is intrinsic to the learning experience in the various fields of study and is presented objectively.

Also, as part of the curriculum, students may be asked to read selections from sacred writings for their literary and historical qualities, but not for devotional purposes. The approach to religion shall be one of instruction, not one of indoctrination. The purpose is to educate, not convert. The focus shall be on the study of what all people believe and must not be on teaching a student what to believe.

At all levels, the study of religious music as part of a musical appreciation course, as a musical experience, as part of a study of various lands and cultures is to be encouraged. Seasonally appropriate religious music may be studied during the season when interest is the highest. In all public school programs and study, care must be taken to avoid presentation of the music as a celebration of a particular religion or religious holiday, and to ensure that there is no bias shown for or against any religion or non-religion.

Schools may teach civic virtues, including honesty, good citizenship, sportsmanship, courage, respect for the rights and freedoms of others, respect for persons and their property, civility, the virtues of moral conviction, tolerance and hard work. Although schools may teach *about* the role religion may play in character and values formation, schools may not invoke religious authority.

Religious Symbolism

Religious messages on T-shirts and the like may not be singled out for suppression. Students may wear religious attire, such as yarmulkes and head scarves, and they may not be forced to wear gym clothes that they regard, on religious grounds, as immodest.

The use of religious symbols that are a part of religious holidays at the appropriate times of the year are permitted teaching aids or as resources, provided such symbols are displayed as examples of the broad cultural and religious heritage of the celebration and are limited to a brief or temporary period of instruction.

School Ceremonies and Activities

School officials may not mandate, organize, or encourage prayer at graduation or other school activities or dedications, nor may they organize a religious baccalaureate ceremony. The school district may rent facilities under the School Communities

Facilities to community groups who wish to sponsor such events. At certain occasions at which it is appropriate to set a solemn tone, a time of silence may be appropriate.

Parents' Right to Excuse Students for Religious Reasons

Students will be excused, when feasible, from lessons/activities that their parents find objectionable for various reasons. Alternative assignments should be substituted.

> Contact: Dr. Joseph Annicharico, Asst. Supt.
> Ramona Unified School District
> 720 Ninth Street
> Ramona, CA 92065
> (619) 788-5145
> (619) 789-9168 (fax)

Appendix B

Calendar of Religious Holidays, 1997/1998

This listing of religious holidays is not exhaustive but is intended to include those major events most likely to be observed by students from a given religious tradition. An explanation of the meaning of these holidays will be found under "Practices" within the chapter on the religion.

The National Conference (formerly the National Conference of Christians and Jews) publishes yearly a "Calendar of Holidays and Festivals," which is distributed through its local offices in major cities throughout the country. It is very comprehensive, and we recommend its use by schools.

1997

January

January 1
Feast of St. Basil (O)

January 6
Epiphany Festival—The Three Kings (C)
El Dia de los Reyes Magnos (RC)

January 7
The Nativity of Jesus Christ (O)

January 10
Ramadan (30 days) (I)

January 13
Maghi (S)

January 15
Birthday of Guru Gobind (S)
Birthday of Rev. Martin Luther
    King Jr. (Af)

1998

January

January 1
Feast of St. Basil (O)

January 6
Epiphany Festival—The Three Kings (C)
El Dia de los Reyes Magnos (RC)

January 7
The Nativity of Jesus Christ (O)

January 15
Birthday of Guru Gobind (S)
Birthday of Rev. Martin Luther
    King Jr. (Af)

January 28
Chinese, Korean, and Vietnamese
    New Year (Year of the Tiger) (B)

January 29
'Id al-Fitr (I)

February

February 7
Chinese, Korean, and Vietnamese
  New Year (Year of the Ox) (B)

February 9
'Id al-Fitr (I)

February 10
Sri Ramakrishna Jayanti (H)

February 11
Vasant Panchami (H)

February 12
Ash Wednesday (Lent begins) (RC, P)

February 15
Nirvâna Day (B)

February 23
Holî (H)

February

February 15
Nirvâna Day (B)

February 25
Ash Wednesday (Lent begins) (RC, P)

February 28
Sri Ramakrishna Jayanti (H)

March

March 10
First day of Lent (O)

March 17
St. Patrick's Day (RC)

March 21
Naw Ruz (Ba)

March 23
Purim (J)
Palm Sunday (RC, P)

March 25
Annunciation (C)

March 27
Maundy/Holy Thursday (RC, P)

March 28
Good Friday (RC, P)

March 30
Easter (RC, P)

March

March 2
First day of Lent (O)

March 12
Purim (J)
Holî (H)

March 17
St. Patrick's Day (RC)

March 21
Naw Ruz (Ba)

March 25
Annunciation (C)

April

April 8
Bikaramajit (H)
Wesak (B)

April 13
Vaisakhi (S)
New Year's Day (B)

April 16
Râma-navami (H)

April 18
'Id al-Adha (I)

April 20
Palm Sunday (O)

April 21
First day of Ridvan (12 days) (Ba)

April 22, 23
First, second days of Passover
   (8 days) (J)

April 24
Armenian Martyrs' Day (O)

April 25
Holy Friday (O)

April 27
Easter (O)

April

April 5
Palm Sunday (RC, P)
Râma-navami (H)

April 8
'Id al-Adha (I)
Wesak (B)

April 9
Maundy Thursday (RC, P)

April 10
Good Friday (RC, P)

April 11, 12
First, second days of Passover (8 days) (J)

April 12
Easter (RC, P)
Palm Sunday (O)

April 13
Vaisakhi (S)
New Year's Day (B)

April 17
Holy Friday (O)

April 19
Easter (O)

April 21
First day of Ridvan (12 days) (Ba)

April 23
Yom Hashoah (J)

April 24
Armenian Martyrs' Day (O)

April 27
Muharram (I)

May

May 4
Yom Hashoah (J)

May 8
Ascension Day (RC, P)
Muharram (I)

May 18
Pentecost (RC, P)

May

May 21
Ascension Day (RC, P)

May 28
Ascension Day (O)

May 31
Shavout (2 days) (J)
Pentecost (RC, P)

June

June 5
Ascension Day (O)

June 9
Martyrdom of Guru Arjan (S)

June 11
Shavout (2 days) (J)

June 15
Pentecost (O)

June 24
Nativity of St. John the Baptist (RC, P)

June

June 7
Pentecost (O)

June 24
Nativity of St. John the Baptist (RC, P)

July

July 9
Martyrdom of the Bab (Ba)

July 17
Ma'uled Al-Nabi (I)

July 24
Pioneer Day (M)

July

July 6
Ma'uled Al-Nabi (I)

July 9
Martyrdom of the Bab (Ba)

July 24
Pioneer Day (M)

August

August 15
Assumption/Feast of the Blessed Virgin
  Mary (RC, O)

August 18
Rakhi (H, Ja)

August 25
Krishna Janmashtami (H)

August

August 8
Rakhi (H, Ja)

August 15
Assumption/Feast of the Blessed Virgin
  Mary (RC, O)
Krishna Janmashtami (H)

September

September 1
Orthodox New Year (O)

September

September 1
Orthodox New Year (O)

September 21
Rosh HaShanah (2 days) (J)

September 28
Confucius Birthday (Cn)

September 28
Confucius Birthday (Cn)

September 30
Yom Kippur (J)

October

October 2
Rosh HaShanah (2 days) (J)

October 11
Dusserah (H, Ja)
Yom Kippur (J)

October 16
Sukkot (7 days) (J)

October 20
Birth of the Bab (Ba)

October 24
Simchat Torah (J)

October 30
Dîwâlî (H, S, Ja)

October 31
Reformation Day (P)

October

October 5
Sukkot (7 days) (J)

October 13
Simchat Torah (J)

October 20
Birth of the Bab (Ba)

October 31
Reformation Day (P)

November

November 1
All Saints Day (RC, P)

November 2
El Dia de los Muertos (RC)

November 12
Birth of Baha'u'llah (Ba)

November 14
Guru Nânak's Birthday (S)

November 30
First Sunday of Advent (C)

November

November 1
Dusserah (H, Ja)
All Saints Day (RC, P)

November 2
El Dia de los Muertos (RC)

November 4
Guru Nânak's Birthday (S)

November 12
Birth of Baha'u'llah (Ba)

November 19
Dîwâlî (H, S, Ja)

November 29
First Sunday of Advent (C)

December

December 4
Martyrdom of Guru Tegh Bahadur Ji (S)

December 6
St. Nicholas Day (C)

December 8
Immaculate Conception (RC)
Bodhi Day (B)

December 12
Feast of Our Lady of Guadalupe (RC)

December 16–24
Las Posadas (RC)

December 24
Hanukkah (8 days) (J)

December 25
Christmas (C)

December 26
Kwanzaa (7 days) (Af)

December 31
Ramadan (30 days) (I)

December

December 6
St. Nicholas Day (C)

December 8
Immaculate Conception (RC)
Bodhi Day (B)

December 12
Feast of Our Lady of Guadalupe (RC)

December 14
Hanukkah (8 days) (J)

December 16–24
Las Posadas (RC)

December 20
Ramadan (30 days) (I)

December 25
Christmas (C)

December 26
Kwanzaa (7 days) (Af)

Key to Religious Groups

Af	African American Christianity
Ba	Baha'i Faith
B	Buddhism
C	Christianity (general)
Cn	Confucianism
H	Hinduism
I	Islam
J	Judaism
Ja	Jainism
M	Mormonism
O	Orthodox Christianity
P	Protestant Christianity
RC	Roman Catholic Christianity
S	Sikhism

Subject Index

141

Art and art classes, xxi, 90
Artemidorus, 110
Articles of Faith (Smith), 49
Aryan Nations, 78
Asalha Puja, 8
Ascension Day, 33
Ascetic practices
    in Buddhism, 10
    in Jainism, 92, 93–94, 95
Ashoka, 10
Ash Wednesday, 33, 67, 69
Assemblies of God, 36, 62
Assemblies of the Called Out Ones of Yah, 45
Assemblies of Yah, 45
Assemblies of Yahweh, 45, 72
Assembly of Yahweh, 45
Assumption, 67
Assyrian Church, 56
Astrology, 5, 111
    and Hinduism, 81
    Jain writings on, 93
Ataturk, 88
Atheists, 117. *See also* Secular Humanism/
        Atheism
August
    religious holidays and festivals during, 138
Aura reading, 111
Aurobindo Ghose, 83
Avolokiteshvara, 11
Awake!, 43
Azerbayjan
    Shi'a Muslims in, 88

Babism, 1
Baby-naming ceremony
    in Judaism, 98
Baha'i Faith, xix, 1–3, 15
    beliefs within, 2
    common misunderstandings/stereotypes
        about, 3
    main subgroups within, 3
    nine-pointed star of, 1
    origins of, 1
    population data on, 3
    practices in, 2–3
    sacred books/scriptures of, 2
Baha'u'llah, 1, 2, 3
Bahrain
    Shi'a Muslims in, 88
Baptism
    in African American Christianity, 36
    Christian, 32
    by immersion, 71
    and Jehovah's Witnesses, 44

    Mormon, 50, 51
    Orthodox Christian, 55, 66
    Protestant view of, 60
    Roman Catholic, 66
    in Sikhism, 120, 121
Baptist church, 60, 64
Baptists, 35, 58
Bar Mitzvah, 98
Barton, Clara, 126
Baruch (Bible, Old Testament), 55, 60, 67
Basil (Saint), 110
    Eucharistic style of, 55
Bat mitzvah, 98
Battle of Armageddon, 43
Bel and the Dragon (Apocrypha), 55, 60, 67
Beliefs, xvii–xviii
    in African American Christianity, 35
    in Baha'i Faith, 2
    in Buddhism, 5–6
    in Christianity, 32
    in Christian Science, 38–39
    in Confucianism, 20–22
    in Fundamentalism, 76–77
    in Hinduism, 81
    in Islam, 86
    in Jainism, 92–93
    of Jehovah's Witnesses, 43–44
    in Judaism, 97–98
    in Mormonism/Church of Jesus Christ
        of Latter-day Saints, 48
    in Native American religions, 102–103
    in New Age religion, 109
    in Orthodox Christianity, 54–55
    in Protestantism, 59
    in Roman Catholicism, 65–66
    in Secular Humanism/Atheism, 117
    of Seventh-day Adventists, 70
    in Sikhism, 120
    in Taoism, 27–28
    in Unitarian Universalism, 124
Benevolence (*jen*), 20
Besant, Annie, 108
Bhagavad Gita, 63, 81, 83
Bhaishajyaguru, 12
Bhutan
    Buddhism in, 13
Bible, the, xviii
    and African American Christianity, 35
    Christian Science view of, 41, 60
    evangelical Christians and, 76
    fundamentalist interpretation of, 75, 76,
        77, 78
    Hebrew, 98
    Islamic ideas about, 87
    and Jehovah's Witnesses, 44, 46

Voting
  Jehovah's Witnesses' view of, 44, 45

Wang Che, 29
Wang Yeh of Taiwan, 18
War, moral views on, xxii, 12, 71, 89
Warring States period
  and Taoism, 25, 26
Washington, George, 116
Washo tribe, 103
Watchtower, The, 43
Watchtower Bible and Tract Society of
    Pennsylvania, The, 43, 44
Way and Its Power, The (Lao Tzu), 16
Way of Confucius, 16
Wesak, 8
Western Heaven of Happiness, 23
Western Paradise, 7, 9, 12
Wheel of dharma, 4
Whirling Dervishes, 88
White, Ellen, 70, 71, 72, 73
White, James, 70
White Painted Woman, 104
Wisdom, 5
Wisdom of Solomon (Apocrypha), 55, 60, 67
Wisdom Sûtras, 7
Witchcraft, 78
Women
  and Baha'i faith, 2, 3
  and Buddhism, 17
  in Jainism, 95
  in Mormonism, 50
  Muslim, 87, 89
  in Taoist society, 26
World Almanac and Book of Facts
  on Buddhist population, 13
  on Chinese folk religionists, 30
  on Confucian population, 24
  on Secular Humanists/Atheists, 118
  on Sikh population, 123

Worldwide Church of God, 72
Worldwide fundamentalism
  characteristics of, 76–77
Worship
  African American Christian, 35
  ancestor, 16, 20, 23
  Baha'i Faith, 2
  in Chinese folk religion, 18
  Christian, 32, 60, 72
  Christian Science, 39
  freedom of, 63
  Hindu, 81, 82
  Islamic, 87
  Jainism, 94
  Quaker, 62
  and questions of morality, xxii
  Taoist, 29
  Unitarian Universalist, 125
Writings, The (Hebrew Bible), 32, 98
Wu, 26

Yahweh, 97
Yahweh's Assembly in Messiah, 45
Yâna, 9
Yarmulke, 98
Yashodâ, 92
Yellow Turbans, 29
Yin-yang, 21–22, 27
  symbol of, 25
Yoga
  in Hinduism, 6
Yom Kippur (Day of Atonement), 99
Young, Brigham, 48

Zen Buddhism, 9, 13
"Zero tolerance" weapons policy, 122
Zoroastrianism/Parsees, xx

About the Authors

Benjamin J. Hubbard is professor and chair of the Department of Religious Studies, California State University, Fullerton, where he has taught since 1985. His specialties include Jewish Studies, Biblical Studies, and Religion and the Media. He received his Ph. D. in religion from the University of Iowa, M.A.s in both theology and journalism from Marquette University, and a B.A. in education from Seattle University.

His previous books include: *Reporting Religion: Facts and Faith* (editor; Sonoma, CA: Polebridge Press, 1990); *Anxiety, Guilt and Freedom: Religious Studies Perspectives* (coeditor; Lanham, MD: University Press of America, 1990); and *The Abraham Connection: A Jew, Christian and Muslim in Dialogue* (coeditor; Notre Dame, IN: Crossroads Books, 1994).

Dr. Hubbard has also taught at Marquette University and St. Jerome's College, University of Waterloo, Ontario. In 1982–83, he was associate editor of the *Wisconsin Jewish Chronicle*. He is a frequent contributor to the *Los Angeles Times*.

161

John T. Hatfield is professor emeritus of Ethnic and Women's Studies and Philosophy, California State Polytechnic University, Pomona. He taught at McGill University and Northern Arizona University before coming to Cal Poly in 1970. He has special interests in Native American Religions and Religion and Education. He is a past president of the American Academy of Religion's Western Region (1996) and of the Far Western Philosophy of Religion Society (1992–94). He received his Ph.D. in religion from the Claremont Graduate School, an M.Th. from the School of Theology at Claremont, and a B.A. in human relations from Palos Verdes College.

He has written several articles on religion and education, and edited (with Benjamin J. Hubbard) a volume on the same subject, *Presence and Promise* (Long Beach: California State University Press, 1992).

James A. Santucci is professor of Religious Studies in the Department of Religious Studies, California State University, Fullerton. From 1970 to 1994, he held a joint appointment in both the Departments of Religious Studies and Linguistics. His specialties include the religions of South Asia (Buddhism, Hinduism, and Jainism), Vedic Studies, Sanskrit, and Modern Religious Movements. He received his Ph.D. in Asian civilizations at the Australian National University, an M.A. in Asian studies at the University of Hawaii, and a B.A. in history at Iona College.

He is editor of the quarterly journal *Theosophical History* and the series *Theosophical History Occasional Papers*. His publications include: *An Outline of Vedic Literature*; *Hindu Art in South and Southeast Asia*; *The Sanskrit Verb (âkhyâtam): The Conjugational System in Classical Sanskrit*; and *The Cave Temples of India: A Photographic Exhibit*.

More Great Books!
from *Teacher Ideas Press*

SERIOUS ILLNESS IN THE CLASSROOM: An Educator's Resource
Andrea L. Mesec
Charles H. Fraser, M.D., Medical Advisor

This resource provides a wealth of information that educators need to support a child within the classroom who has a health problem. The authors describe each condition, discuss common treatments, explain the process of diagnosis, and list symptoms and warning signs. Lesson plans based on serious illnesses allow educators to teach students about the conditions.
xv, 117p. paper ISBN 1-56308-416-3

APPRECIATING DIVERSITY THROUGH CHILDREN'S LITERATURE:
Teaching Activities for the Primary Grades
Meredith McGowan, Patricia J. Wheeler, and Tom McGowan

Incorporating literature about diverse people into the curriculum encourages students to comprehend and value diversity. In this resource, stories that focus on four areas of diversity—age, gender, physical abilities, and ethnicity—provide the basis for activities that encourage children to think, empathize, and take action. **Grades 1–3**.
xvii, 135p. 8½x11 paper ISBN 1-56308-117-2

EXPLORING DIVERSITY: Literature Themes and Activities for Grades 4–8
Jean E. Brown and Elaine C. Stephens

Take the riches of multicultural literature beyond the printed page and into the classroom. With a variety of themes, discussion questions, and activities that challenge misconceptions and stereotypes, this book gives students the opportunity to develop an understanding of and appreciation for their own and other cultures. **Grades 4–8**.
x, 210p. 8½x11 paper ISBN 1-56308-322-1

THE INTERNET RESOURCE DIRECTORY
FOR K–12 TEACHERS AND LIBRARIANS, 96/97 Edition
Elizabeth B. Miller

This award-winning annual offers you access to current, accurate, useful information about the network. Designed for educators with annotated and screened sites, it organizes material by curriculum areas.
paper ca. 250p. ISBN 1-56308-506-2

For a FREE catalog or to place an order, please contact:

Teacher Ideas Press
Dept. B40 · P.O. Box 6633 · Englewood, CO 80155-6633
1-800-237-6124, ext. 1 · Fax: 303-220-8843 · E-mail: lu-books@lu.com
Web site: www.lu.com/tip